Praise for the Breaking Thro

This book is a practical roadmap that should be read by all those whose passion is serving clients and building truly exceptional and sustainable entrepreneurial enterprises. I've been in this industry for a long time, and have proudly worked with thousands of advisors. There is a reason why so few advisors reach the $10 million in annual revenue that Tim and his team reached. This book tells of what you need to do to be one of those advisors. It speaks to the traits that nearly all successful advisors have—they work on growing their business and setting the standards for how the organization will serve clients rather than the business; they rely on outsourced partners and team members to handle running the business, operations, reporting, compliance, technology, etc.; and they learn from people who have successfully scaled to grow the business.

Tim has experienced success in this industry across every business model, from full service employee advisor to RIA. His hands-on experience in building total enterprise value for himself, his partners, and his family has specific lessons for anyone looking to take their business to the next level.

Jamie Price
President and CEO, Advisor Group

I had the privilege of working closely with Tim and Max for over two years as they provided critical guidance in the growth of our financial planning practice. As a relatively new company, led by innovative and entrepreneurial founders without a vast experience in the space, our leadership team yearned for experienced wisdom to ensure that we scaled in a way that could bless our team and our clients. We wanted to work with someone that has been there, done that.

We are so thankful to have met Tim and Max. They have a willingness to dig into any aspect of this business with obvious competence. They are passionate in ensuring that the people that they work with learn from their history, and build a business that will bring peace. It is very challenging to find insight within all aspects of the business from one source. Tim and Max can bring practical insight to the overall vision of a company, how to attract clients, how to serve current clients through proven meeting strategies, building investment platforms, financial planning, serving high-net worth clientele, operations, finance, technology … the list goes on and on.

I am encouraged that they decided to put the methodologies to pen and paper, and now a resource is available for those looking to scale their financial planning businesses. I have no doubt that this book will be a valuable resource to all that utilize it.

Justin Ross

President, Accelerated Wealth, LLC

Providing advice to wealthy clients and institutions is always a complicated problem or opportunity. The larger the assets the more complexity and frustration impacts sound decision making. All clients will choose simplicity over complexity, especially if a board is involved or if family dynamics play a major role. Advisors need to learn to navigate complexity and realize it is an opportunity to strengthen the relationship by just saying "yes" to complexity and simplifying the client's life. This amazing book teaches you how to say "yes" and grow your business by serving your clients better.

Michael T. Dieschbourg

Head, Responsibility and Stewardship Office, North America,
Hermes Responsibility and Stewardship Company
Former director of institutional consulting, Citigroup
Former board member, Investment & Wealth Institute

I watched Tim and Max walk out the path from wire house to independent RIA to the sale of the firm, so I know the numbers are real. What is most powerful however is not their success but rather their willingness to teach from their mistakes (also real). I plan to put a copy of this book into the hands of every one of my FA CEO clients and FA firm leader friends.

Steve Simpson

ChristianCEO.net

I have been in the financial services industry since 1981 calling on wire houses and RIAs. Every week I am asked by a team how other FAs are growing their businesses since they have "hit the wall." This is the first book in thirty-five years that FAs can read and understand how to increase assets!

Bill Ikard

Vice president, Advisory Research, Inc.

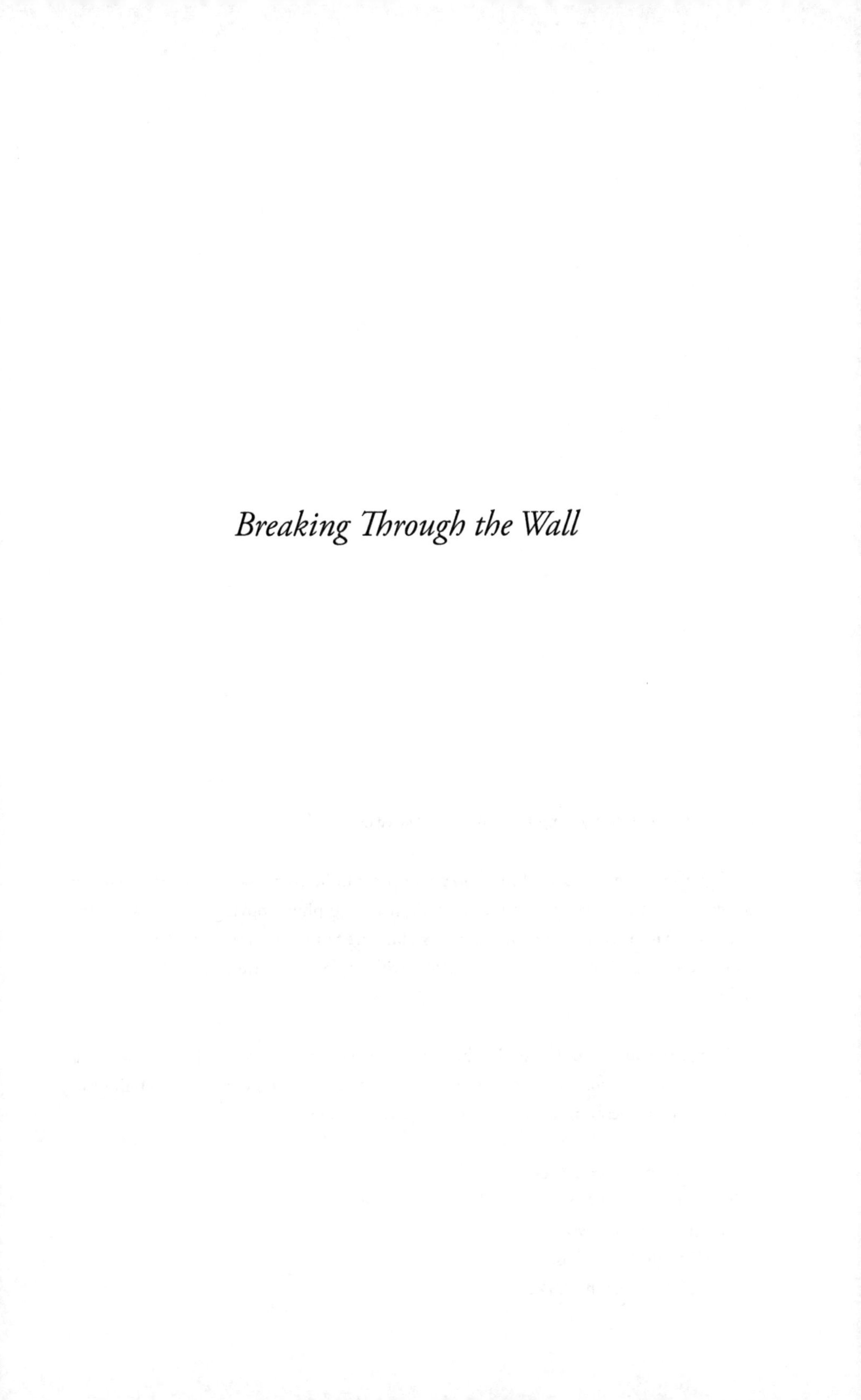

Breaking Through the Wall

Printed in the United States of America.
Library of Congress Control Number: 2020902965
ISBN: 978-1-94963-951-3
Cover Design: Jamie Wise
Layout Design: Sarah Durkee

Breaking Through THE WALL

A Financial Advisor's Guide to Grow, Scale, and Monetize Your Business for Millions

Timothy Kneen & Maxwell Smith

DEDICATION

Timothy Kneen: To my wife, Gretchen, for allowing me to fail and for blindly supporting me every day, every hour, and every moment because you believed. The power you give us is immeasurable.

Thanks, G.

To my father for the spirit of being an entrepreneur. You always said, *Work harder than anyone else can imagine so you can spend the rest of your life enjoying it like few can.*

Thanks, Dad.

Maxwell Smith: To my mentor in life and business, Timothy Kneen. Your faith, belief, and guidance has brought me a wealth of knowledge that cannot be replaced. Thank you for always supporting me through the thick and thin.

CONTENTS

ABOUT THE AUTHORS

Timothy Kneen

Tim began providing financial consulting services to institutional investors and select families over thirty years ago. He began at Dean Witter and became one of the youngest vice presidents in its history. He went on to enjoy a twenty-plus year career with Citigroup, where he became a director with Citi Institutional Consulting. Just before Citigroup became owned primarily by the US government, the United Bank of Switzerland (UBS) recruited Tim and his team.

He later founded IFAM Capital with his longtime partner Clayton Hartman and grew that firm into one of top one hundred registered advisory firms/wealth management firms in the country as measured by Fidelity. During those years, Tim lead the firm's ultra-high net worth individuals and institutional practices, including investment methodologies such as the "Known Return" portfolio, and lead business development for the firm. At his retirement, IFAM was billing in excess of $10 million in annual revenue and was managing well over a billion dollars. Having moved between wire-house firms, then to independence, and then successfully transitioning that firm to the next generation of advisors within the firm, he has grown a firm from a few hundred thousand in annual revenue to over $10 million using both organic and inorganic (acquisition related) growth. Tim is known for being able to look outside the box for solutions.

While at IFAM, Tim and his team received numerous awards. He was elected president of the Association of Professional Investment Consultants (APIC) and has served as chair on both the association's research and evaluation committee and the conference committee. He was awarded APIC's highest honor, the Tom Gorman Award, to acknowledge his service to the industry. Tim was also named one of the top forty young entrepreneurs in *Denver Business Journal*'s prestigious "40 Under 40" list. *Barron's* recognized him both as one of the "Top 100 Consultants in America" and one of the "Top 1,000 Advisors." He was also named as the number one consultant in Colorado by the *Denver Business Journal*, the premier advisor for financial planning from the National Association of Board Certified Advisory Practices, and as one of the top consultants by *Research* magazine.

Just before Tim left IFAM, the firm was acquired by Focus Financial Partners to become one of the thirty original partner-level firms that form the now publicly traded Focus Financial Partners.

Tim is a regular speaker at national conferences, a published author, and is regularly interviewed in the media on topics related to the economy and investing.

Tim is active away from financial services as well. He has started or bought seven different businesses ranging from manufacturing to apparel, from technology to real estate development, and from private club management to financial services—ultimately selling two to financial buyers, two to synergistic buyers, and taking one public.

Today Tim continues to share these real-life experiences with other business owners and financial consultants across the country through private consulting and speaking engagements with his firm Lumina Consulting. Recently Lumina helped a firm scale from less that $2 million in annual fee-based revenue to over $9 million, proving that not only can he build his own firm but he can also build others' firms.

Tim completed his undergraduate work at the University of Denver and received his CIMA® certification from his work, sponsored through the Investment Management Consultants Association, at the Wharton School of Business at the University of Pennsylvania.

Tim is involved with his church, as well as with several local and national charities. He has cofounded and chaired events, including the Red Lady Ball, the Denver Victims Rock and Roll, Sunrise Africa, SaddleUp! Foundation, and many other events. He enjoys golf, skiing, tennis, and mountain climbing, among many other sports. Tim is married with three children and resides at Colorado Golf Club.

Maxwell Smith

Max has over a decade of experience working within the financial services industry. Formerly Max managed the marketing and sales, as well as assisted with operations and research, for a senior institutional team at the United Bank of Switzerland (UBS). In 2014, he helped lead the transition with Focus Financial Partners to move the team to independence in creating IFAM Capital. He assisted in building and onboarding their platform and created the firm's marketing collateral in addition to developing the firm's sales and marketing plans.

Upon IFAM's opening, Max helped advisors implement and develop their sales processes and marketing strategies, and performed portfolio analytics and created financial plans for prospective and incoming clients. In addition to this, he led the merger and acquisition team and chaired the firm's marketing committee. He helped in the building of an internal asset management platform for IFAM and led the transition of multiple tuck-ins, helping the firm grow nearly 50 percent in revenue during that time. He also assisted in developing the firm's and their advisors' growth strategies both organically and inorganically. Max has consulted for other registered investment advisors (RIAs) in regard to organic growth strategies, succession planning, merger and acquisition strategies, as well as operational and platform guidance.

Today Max applies his experience and expertise working for a top one hundred-ranked RIA in the country and acts as a consultant for wire-house advisors looking at the break-away process and for established independent financial advisory practices looking to create their own unique growth strategies, create succession plans, and develop operational efficiency to be able to increase productivity.

Having been a part of close to $2 billion worth of acquisitions/mergers, Max has a keen insight to assisting firms looking to get into merger and acquisitions. He assists them in developing M&A strategies and provides assistance in firm due diligence, proforma creations, valuations, deal structures, as well as transition and tuck-in consulting post-closing.

Max currently lives in Denver, Colorado, and enjoys skiing, golfing, and hiking.

CHAPTER 1
THE THINGS WE WISH WE'D KNOWN

Many advisors out there are facing a wall. They're generating $1-3 million in revenue. They're servicing all the households they think they can possibly manage. They have little time to spend with their families or do all the other things that are important to them. They are chief marketing officer, chief investment officer, head of meetings with clients, head of overseeing operational problems, CEO, CFO, chief compliance officer, chief technology officer, etc. There just aren't enough hours in the day.

This book is an insider's look into how to get past that wall. With a combined forty-five years of experience standing in your shoes, this book is about sharing all the failures we had and the resulting success on how to get past that wall. After navigating each phase of the industry ourselves—from wire house, to RIA, to buying other RIAs, to monetizing half of our firm—we understand what it takes to succeed. Yet there are so many things we *wish* we'd known when we were trying to grow.

We faced a $1-2 million wall ourselves, then another wall around $4 million, and we made many mistakes trying to overcome both. We learned what works from real-life experience. Like we did, you can develop a practice with $1 billion or more in assets under management that generates $10 million or more in gross revenue—and ultimately sell half of that firm for $20 million or more. We've been there and done that, and we'll show you how to get there.

Why This Book

There are so many books about how to build a practice with $100 million in assets under management, which yields around $1 million in revenue (at a 1 percent fee). This, while producing a good living, is only a beginning in our industry today; at many wire houses, average production is now around $1 million.[1] The big players in our industry are doing at least $10 million in revenue, while many advisors reach $1-2 million and can't figure out how to go higher. That's why there are so many books about how to grow a financial advisory business.

We read a lot of them. After just a few, we started looking more closely at who these authors were. What were their qualifications to tell us how to run our business? Why were we reading another book saying what we already knew, just in different words? We were already successful in the industry, so if these authors weren't *more* successful, why were we listening to them? This is the book we were looking for back then—a book written by financial advisors who had done exactly what we wanted to do.

We're trying to tell an important story *and* help you avoid the mistakes we made. In fact, this is the exact story we wish we'd been told when we were facing the wall.

If you want to have a business that has gross revenue of $1-2 million, then put this book down and pick up any of the other hundreds of books on the subject written by people who never built a financial advisory business beyond that level.

But if you want a business that produces millions in *net* income instead of gross—one that you can sell half of for $20 million or more—then keep reading.

---

1 "Morgan Stanley FA Production Surpasses Merrill Lynch," Financial Advisor IQ, January 19, 2017, https://financialadvisoriq.com/c/1545173/174633.

Asking Why and Becoming an Entrepreneur

Advisors get stuck in their early years just going out and acquiring new clients. They become machines doing that. They need to slow down and ask *why*—why are you doing this, and what is it you want to be?

Asking why is critical because you must make a decision that will determine your future trajectory: Are you building a business or a lifestyle model? An advisor building a lifestyle model is saying, "I'm going to make a decent living and just do what I do. I'm going to show up at work at 9:30 a.m. and be home at 3:00 p.m. because I want to play golf or see my kid's game three times a week." That decision limits you to doing roughly $1 million in revenue and making $300K-$400K net. There is nothing wrong with that, but if that is your goal then this book is not for you!

If you're building a business, you have to actively decide to be an entrepreneur, which means you're going to work lots of hours. You're going to live and breathe your business. You're going to drive the people around you. You're going to become a business owner, not just an advisor. If you're building this kind of business, you need to turn to those who have been there and done that. Watch and study what they have done. Learn from their successes and their mistakes.

Learning from Real-Life Experience

Advisors hitting the wall need to learn from more experienced advisors who are generating more revenue, investing better, and running better businesses. In short, you need to understand the model of how to get bigger. Our knowledge about how to grow a FA business is a result of our own experience—having looked for the right way, made mistakes, and ultimately found the right solutions. But to know this, we had to seek out people who were doing more business and running better businesses.

This book is about sharing with you not only how we grew the business and all the hurdles we had along the way, but it's also about some of the things we financial advisors think when we have been in the business for a while: Am I at the right place to do the best for my clients and to maximize the future value of my work? We didn't know this answer for sure either! In fact, some of the answers we found were the wrong ones. We moved from wire house to wire house, from a wire house to independence, and from being independent to acquiring other independents. We even took the last step in deciding how to monetize the work we had done by selling half of our firm for more than $20 million. We use this real-life experience to share how you can make some of these decisions as well.

While it sounds like we did so much right, what this book is really about is all the mistakes that we made along the way. We wanted to write this book to share what we've learned so entrepreneurial advisors can avoid making the same mistakes. With the knowledge we have now, there are so many things we would have done differently. Our goal is to help advisors avoid making those mistakes or at least to educate them so that they can make better decisions.

Here's what's to come in the following chapters:

Chapter 2: What You Need to Succeed

Using data from the major custodians' annual benchmarking studies, we begin this chapter discussing what high performance looks like. We then talk about the key attributes of advisors who get to this high-performing level. Let's cover those briefly now:

Ability to scale: You need to go from being the shopper, chief cook, and dishwasher to being a singular role player on a team. You simply cannot do everything—you *must* build a team around you and become the thought leader while your team handles the day-to-day. There's truly no way to become a big player in this industry if you continue to do everything yourself. If you want to grow, you need a team to support you. The key is how to do it!

Establishing a specialty: How do investors decide whether to hire one firm over another? They hire the firm that specializes in exactly what they need. Our niche was helping clients monetize their business and set up a family office. Clients are looking for advisors who are specialists in something and unique in their approach. Running financial plans and selecting from other people's investment ideas won't get you to the next level. Sure, it may get you a start in the business; it may even get you to $1-2 million in revenue. But it won't allow you to achieve the goals of this book. You must have a niche! The key is how you become a specialist!

Ability to remove client anxiety over money: It doesn't matter what else we do right; we will ultimately be judged by our investment performance and our ability to bring peace where financial anxiety exists. When a client is facing financial anxiety, he or she wants reassurance. Ideally, every young advisor should get drilled on case studies for months before they ever sit in front of a client. Then, they should sit second chair to a senior advisor who shows them how to create peace in a client facing financial anxiety. This is not innate. It is learned. The key is to learn from those who have sat in that chair.

Being connected to new business or outworking the competition: For more than three decades, the advisors who make it big are either already connected to sources of clients or they outwork the competition—or both. It has been the case for thirty years and is still true today. The key is to make sure your hard work is placed in the right areas so you make your closing rate increase after finding new opportunities.

Self-confidence: High-performing advisors have a deep-seated belief in how *they* invest money and the value they provide to the client. This attitude comes across in how they tell their story. Advisors also need a healthy ego because rejection and getting yelled at come with the territory of being a financial advisor. The key is that you must honestly believe in what you do and how you do it. If you don't yet have that belief, you have to learn from others until you really do believe because all $10 million-dollar advisors have this trait.

Integrity: This business attracts many high-ego people, but the best ones also have an unusual quality of high integrity. We are aware that the media suggests otherwise, yet we rarely see a lead advisor on a high-performing team who doesn't have deep integrity. He or she *always* puts clients first. The key is to believe that it will be acceptable to lose money in order to do the right thing for your client!

Conviction: There is no certain outcome to investments. We all know this. The advisors who truly believe in what they're doing—despite the built-in uncertainty of the business—are the ones who build high-performing teams and create conviction among their teammates. This conviction is key because your staff needs to believe in you as much as your clients.

Knowing yourself: You want to be meeting with prospects and clients when you're at your peak. Knowing yourself and when you work best is critical to growing. The key is to build a schedule where you can remain healthy and at peak performance when you need to be!

Chapter 3: The Best of the Best

Why figure it out on your own when you can learn from the best advisors out there? In this chapter, we profile some of the best advisors in the industry who acted as the advisors we learned from. But first, we discuss niche in more detail. What are your options for specializing? You might focus on physicians, executives with complicated benefits packages, or foundations and endowments—among many others. Whatever it is, once you have selected what you will be a specialist in, you need to invest in your education and market yourself as a specialist. That's what all of the best of the best advisors have done. You also need to surround yourself with a group of industry peers. We joined the Association of Professional Investment Consultants (APIC), and this group was essential to our growth and success. Some APIC members became the people we learned from—just as we are telling you to find more successful advisors to learn from.

Chapter 4: Building the Right Team

We see so many advisors get stuck at the $1-2 million wall because they don't want, or don't have the ability, to build a team around them. To get to where the big players are, you have to build a team. Of the advisors who get this, many make the critical mistake of building a horizontal team. There is no scale—or at least much less scale—in that structure. Instead, build your firm vertically to maximize profits, control, and lifestyle. While the team is servicing clients, you, the senior advisor, can focus on being a subject matter expert and growing the firm.

Relationship managers are the core of the team. They quarterback client relationships and deliver relationship alpha—a higher level of service that, we argue, is even more important than investment alpha. By managing a client's budgets, bill paying, lending, health care, P/C insurance, etc., your firm becomes the center of the client's financial life. With relationship managers in place, the client is not relying on you, the senior advisor. Therefore, you can sell the business for a premium. Clients are going to stay because *you* are not who the relationship is with. Your relationship managers are servicing the clients, building that loyalty, and helping you create an organization that's highly valuable to a prospective buyer.

This chapter also covers how to pay for your team. We believe in fixed salaries instead of variable pay, and we talk about what those numbers look like for relationship managers, operations managers, and other staff.

Chapter 5: The Risks of Partnerships

Many advisors who are stuck at the $1-2 million wall decide to partner. They think one advisor focusing on financial planning and the other on investments allows you to create more revenue. Reality shows otherwise. If an advisor is already facing a wall, then bringing on a partner to do additional services for clients will have marginal impact on income. Standard industry wisdom is that partnering will get you over the wall, yet a high percentage of those partnerships fail. The cost of that failure is much greater than you think. Having been through failed partnerships ourselves, we can tell you what kind of partnerships *do* work and how to structure them. Perhaps most importantly, we can tell you when to avoid them.

Chapter 6: Clearing the Hurdles

You need to be very aware of the hurdles that trip up advisors trying to grow. Chapter 6 discusses these. Number one is building a defensible asset management strategy. You can't just talk about products anymore. You need to believe in an investment philosophy, practice it with your own money, and speak about it with passion. The other hurdles include being a business owner, not just a financial advisor; maintaining price integrity; burning out; and falling in love with an asset manager or specific product. All of these are mistakes we made!

Chapter 7: Running Your Practice Like a Business

Running your practice like a business means understanding the value you provide clients, tracking your business, utilizing tax advantages, planning for a market crash, and having a philosophy around paying your team—all things a thought leader has time to work on with the team structure we teach.

This chapter also talks about family. We believe in working as hard on your family as you do on your business. Sadly, one frequent victim in our industry is marriage. We have one of the highest divorce rates of any profession. It's not hard to understand why: we're under enormous pressure. We work incredible hours. People either love us or hate us, and that can change in a few hours with a market crash. It's just the nature of the business.

Please don't let your entrepreneurial drive cause you to neglect your family. It does not have to. Meg Hirshberg wrote an incredible book about this called *For Better or For Work: A Survival Guide for Entrepreneurs and Their Families*. Look, we *can* be entrepreneurs and have balance. Much of it has to do with structuring your team and how you deal with pressure. This chapter speaks to how we did it and the mistakes we made.

Chapter 8: How to Grow Your Practice

This chapter is all about marketing. You start with a crisp elevator pitch defining your niche. From there, you develop a written marketing plan. We consult with advisors every day and are continually shocked to see how many don't have a written marketing plan. Once you have a plan, you follow it, measure it, and comp it. Comping means aligning compensation with marketing, so bonuses are tied to how the entire organization does in terms of retaining clients and getting new clients. We discuss how to pay for marketing; do not use variable pay. Use the same fixed salary and bonus structure. In this chapter we not only discuss what did and did not work for us but also discuss the practices of other advisors we have met on our journey.

Chapter 9: How to Grow Through M&A

All the marketing strategies we talk about in Chapter 8 create organic growth. While this type of growth is important, it pales in comparison to inorganic growth—i.e., mergers and acquisitions. M&A is very powerful in our business because you can get hundreds of new clients in a single transaction. But there is a reason 90 percent of M&A is done by people who have done it before: expertise in this area is a prerequisite. We grew our firm through many M&A transactions that increased our assets under management. This chapter covers what it takes to be successful at M&A.

Chapter 10: The Choices You Make

For decades now, the system of "protocol" has allowed the wire houses to steal advisors from one another. The industry is starting to change this, and it's becoming less lucrative for advisors to move from one wire house to another. This means more advisors are setting up their own shops. It also means an opportunity for independents to jump in and acquire talent.

This chapter discusses all the options available, from being a wire house advisor to establishing an independent firm. Wire houses have changed with the dismantling of protocol; independents have changed as well to include semi-independents and partnered indies. An advisor's fundamental choice, however, remains the same: do you want to be an employee, or do you want to be an entrepreneur? This chapter gives you a framework to make decisions and discusses the mistakes we made so you can avoid them.

Do you want to be an employee, or do you want to be an entrepreneur?

Chapter 11: How to Make a Graceful Exit

Most business owners say, "We want to grow to *x* revenue and then exit." Our industry differs. Many financial advisors don't see it that way. They think about growing their revenue, but there is no master plan that we see in other industries. You need to actively plan for the long term because the most critical thing you're going to do for your exit strategy is make yourself irrelevant. Thinking from a client's perspective underscores why: if you're working with an advisor who has all your money and that individual retires, and you're told, "Now you're working with Joe over here," you might stay. You might not. A graceful exit is different. It's one that honors your clients, employees, and partners. It allows you to feel blessed by the people and the process. This chapter is about how you get your ducks in a row to create that kind of exit and what we learned from doing it wrong.

Chapter 12: What is the Future of Our Industry?

In this chapter, we talk about the advisor of the future. We suggest that this advisor will become a financial quarterback for their clients, coordinating more services for the client, and we discuss how this will help the best advisors avoid fee compression.

What you know today will be very different later in your career. A lack of training has been a problem in our industry, but that's slowly changing. Three decades ago, there wasn't anything like an apprentice program for investing. Today, the wire houses and bigger independent firms are having young advisors learn from a successful team. Recruiting and training young advisors is going to see huge changes in the next few decades with America's aging population increasingly in need of help managing their assets. Recruiting and training is likely to become one of the most important things you will have to become proficient at to build the right team around you. We think investment management will become a degree at most major universities, just like accounting and business management.

There are other changes we see happening in our industry as well: wire houses moving to the salary-bonus model over variable pay and limiting advisor discretion in choosing investments. Super-regional independents form as acquisitions increase.

Chapter 13: Winners Make the Most Mistakes

You can't be afraid to fail in this business. The revered basketball coach John Wooden believed that mistakes were the mark of a winner. Sure, sometimes we make a call that doesn't work out. But as Wooden later said, "If you never fail, you weren't trying." We made all the mistakes we're warning against in this book, and we still got to $10 million in revenue. So can you!

A Closing Thought

This business is filled with opportunity and the ability to lead a life that can make a meaningful impact on your clients' lives. But it's not easy. Putting in long hours and having conviction when your decisions get questioned are part of getting big.

This does not mean that you cannot be in a great marriage, be a great parent, and have great hobbies. It does mean you have to take care of yourself. A key source of strength is your health. If you're going to be an entrepreneur, you've got to be in great health. That means you work out persistently. You've got to be doing something that equips your body to handle the stress of this business. It's telling that many of the biggest players in our industry come from an athletics background. Without great health, the pressures of this life will just eat you up.

Besides taking care of our physical health, how did we deal with the pressure, the sacrifices, and still make it work? We built families based on faith. We believe in some sound principles with faith as our cornerstone. As a result, when problems arise we have a backbone to guide us to sound decisions. Where do you find peace? Where do you find conviction? Almost all advisors with $10 million in revenue can answer these questions.

If you're stuck at $1-2 million, out of time, and want to win, this book will show you how to get past that wall. Let's now jump in to Chapter 2 where we define high performance and discuss in more detail the key attributes of all successful advisors.

CHAPTER 2
WHAT YOU NEED TO SUCCEED

Our definition of success is getting past the $1-3 million wall and separating your book of business from the pack. This book is about how to become a high-performing advisor on a high-performing team. This book is not for financial advisors who want to stay in the $1-2 million pack or less, which is exactly where many advisors end up spending their careers.

This book *is* for those advisors who want to be entrepreneurs, separate themselves from that pack, and build a business with $1 billion AUM that you can sell half of for more than $20 million. Success means developing a high-performing team that services more money and nets more revenue with fewer employees—all of which leads to greater levels of growth, productivity, and profitability.

What Does High Performance Look Like?

In Fidelity's RIA Benchmarking Study[2], median high-performing firms (HPFs) had more assets under management and more revenue with fewer full-time employees: $484 million in assets under management for high performers compared to $305 million for all other firms in the category; $3 million in revenue compared to $2 million; and seven

---

2 "Growth, Productivity, and Profitability: Maximize Your RIA Firm's Harvest," *Fidelity*, 2017, https://clearingcustody.fidelity.com/app/proxy/content?literatureURL=/9882273.PDF.

full-time employees compared to nine. Yes, you read that right! Larger firms had fewer employees in the high-performing category. Advisors with HPFs each serve eighty-two clients on average, while advisors with all other firms serve seventy-two clients. Due to high-performing firms' ability to service more clients and attract bigger clients with fewer full-time employees, HPFs earn $813,544 per advisor while revenue per advisor for all other firms in the category is $588,772.

Let's look at the growth numbers in Schwab's RIA Benchmarking Study: "The 5-year net organic growth CAGR of the subset of fastest-growing firms is almost four times that of all other firms—16.2 percent compared with 4.3 percent at the median. This translates into a significant difference in dollars—net organic growth for the fastest-growing firms in 2016 amounted to $51 million, versus $14 million for all other firms."[3] Simply put, we believe advisors who are following the concepts in this book are growing at four times the rate of other firms. And they're not just growing because they're getting more clients; they're growing because they're getting better clients. "These firms are attracting not only more clients but higher-value clients," reads the Schwab study.

A study on high-performing advisor teams[4] agrees with Schwab that AUM distribution is very different for HPFs. Ultrahigh net worth clients ($2 million or more in assets) made up 58 percent of high-performing teams' books of business. For all other firms, it was 26 percent. Top quartile, high-performing teams averaged $280 million AUM per senior advisor while all other firms averaged $60 million. High-performing advisors were therefore handling 4.2*x* the assets of other advisors.

---

3 "2017 RIA Benchmarking Study," *Charles Schwab*, 2017, https://advisorservices.schwab.com/public/advisor/nn/insights_hub/advisors/benchmarking.html.

4 Kenton Shirk, "High-Performing Advisor Teams," *Investments and Wealth Research*, no. 4 (2017), https://investmentsandwealth.org/getmedia/c005b352-ff7a-4cae-8148-225f9b255a88/2017-Q4-InvestmentsWealthResearch-(1).pdf.

When you dig into the data, you see that HPFs manage *more* money and generate *more* revenue with *fewer* people. How do they accomplish this? HPFs have built the right infrastructure so their employees can focus on managing relationships while partners focus on growth and strategic vision. We'll discuss this in detail in Chapter 4, "Building Your Team."

This chapter covers another vital reason why high-performing advisors are able to manage more money and generate more revenue with fewer employees: they possess an arsenal of key personal and professional attributes.

The Eight Key Attributes of HPFs

Ability to scale is the number-one key attribute of high-performing advisors. All high-performing advisors have scaled their business. Bestselling author David Bach understands this and coaches his clients accordingly: "Many advisors don't know how to put teams in place," writes Brad Johnson about Bach's philosophy. "Because they can't scale their individual productivity, they hit a ceiling and don't last. Nobody wants to buy them."[5]

High-performing advisors learn how to grow their business without running out of time. They add the right people around them. They understand that they can't be the center of everything and must give up some control, trusting others to manage the relationships. As a result, they can keep adding clients and still have time to run the business. This book will teach you how to do the same things.

Lots of advisors get to the point where they're making a million in gross revenue and $300Kor $400K in profits. The eight attributes of high-performing advisors we're discussing this chapter—with

5 Brad Johnson, "David Bach Reveals Three Keys to Growing a Multi-Billion RIA," *Wealth Management,* May 10, 2018, http://www.wealthmanagement.com/business-planning/david-bach-reveals-three-keys-growing-multi-billion-ria.

ability to scale being the first and most critical—do not apply to the people who get to $1 million. Those people come in all different shapes and sizes with a different set of traits. The people who get past that level, however, first and foremost understand the idea of scaling. They trust somebody else to run operations, manage clients, do investment research, position portfolios, and lead marketing. We have never seen a single $10 million advisor who hadn't scaled his or her business. This doesn't mean a high-performing advisor doesn't participate in all these activities, but it does mean that he or she lets others be the center of that activity while the advisor focuses on building the firm.

The biggest lesson we wish we had learned at an earlier stage in our career was that we had to scale. We kept thinking we could do everything. We worked ourselves almost to the point of giving up on the business because we were so exhausted and didn't want to invest the money to scale. We didn't want to invest in somebody to lead on the marketing side—or a relationship manager to handle accounts or a client concierge to make sure clients felt special—so we could focus on growing the business.

The biggest lesson we wish we had learned at an earlier stage in our career was that we had to scale.

We kept convincing ourselves not to spend that money and instead do everything ourselves. This caused us to get stuck around $2 million in revenue without the knowledge of how to go bigger. It took us a lot of years to figure this out. We only figured it out by watching other advisors who were bigger than we were. But we could have gotten there ten years earlier had we known what we're teaching here.

Establishing a specialty is the second key attribute. As an investor, how do you decide to hire one firm over another? According to Matt Oechsli, an expert on attracting, servicing, and retaining affluent clients, 71 percent of advisor teams that bring in more than $20 million annually in new assets have a niche.[6] For example, at the firm we built, we specialized in helping clients monetize their life's work. Our clients were selling a business, transitioning it to the next generation, or rewarding the team that helped them build it. We provided them with the expertise to build and sell that individual's company and then transition to their own family office.

How did we back up our claim to that expertise? As we told prospects, it came from personal experience. We talked about the companies we had built and later sold and the different exit strategies we employed—from taking one public to selling one to a private equity firm to selling another to a Fortune 500 company. We talked with prospects about building a family office, what that can mean, and how their lives would change like ours did.

In the next chapter, "The Best of the Best," we'll talk about establishing your specialty because *all* top advisors have carved out a niche.

Ability to remove client anxiety over money is the third key attribute. We all know that money causes anxiety. Think about how many areas of life set off anxiety over money: marriage, a job, a house, retirement, or sending your kids to college. It doesn't matter how much money you have—it's still at the root of much anxiety.

Anybody can write a financial plan. You can go online and do it for yourself. But when you're facing financial anxiety, you want someone who you believe has a higher financial IQ than you telling you that you're okay. That's what high-performing advisors do.

High-performing advisors possess an innate ability to alleviate their clients' anxieties over money. They do that through proper

6 Matt Oechsli, "Which Niches Bring the Most Riches?" *Wealth Management,* June 7, 2018, http://www.wealthmanagement.com/marketing/which-niches-bring-most-riches.

financial planning so they can demonstrate exactly why the client is going to be okay. But what makes these high-performing advisors different from everyone else who just does a financial plan is they are constantly reinforcing to the client why they shouldn't have anxiety.

Removing anxiety is a combination of three things. The first is being available when the client's financial life is in peril. That means you're not waiting for the client to call you—you're calling them. Second is assertiveness. Advisors who can remove client anxiety do not say, "What do you think about this?" They say, "I've been here before, I've seen this before, and here's what you need to do." And the third thing is presence. Advisors with presence—those who have firmly established their expertise—reassure the client because they have been there and done this before.

Being connected to streams of new business or outworking the competition is the fourth key attribute of HPFs. Who is highly connected? CPAs, for example, already have a role in managing their clients' finances. CPAs don't need to go out and find new clients; they know where the money is and are already connected to eligible investors. Other professionals who are connected include auditors, professional fundraisers, sports agents, and estate planners. What about the successful advisors who aren't already connected to streams of new business? Those advisors establish a niche and simply work harder than everyone else. If the average advisor makes *x* efforts to bring in new clients, the high-performing advisor makes 3*x* efforts. In later chapters, we talk about some of the things these advisors do.

Self-confidence is the fifth key attribute of high-performing advisors. We know it sounds horrible, but in this case ego is good. We don't see *any* high-performing advisors who don't have a deep belief in their experience, the service they offer, and how they invest money. High-performing advisors truly believe that they are the best at what they do. You never hear them say to a client, "Here are three choices for you to choose from. What is best for you?"

There are three main reasons why high-performing advisors have to have ego and are so eager to talk about what *they* do, not what *the other guy* does. The first reason is that every high-performing advisor has a story to tell. The second is that they realize they must have an opinion about everything because they are getting paid for their opinion. They don't say the market might go up for these reasons or down for these reasons to hedge their bet. They have an opinion. The client is coming to them for new knowledge, not more of what they already know. Eventually, that opinion will be wrong, and the advisor needs to be okay with being wrong every once in a while, which, let's face it, takes a little ego. And the third reason is that we are in the business of getting turned down. Sometimes you get slapped in the proverbial face, which gets old very quickly if you don't have a healthy ego.

In the early stages of our careers, for every client we landed probably ten turned us down. In the later stages, we would win four out of five new client opportunities. Your batting average does go up—from .100 early in your career to .800 or higher in the later stages—but we're still in the business of getting turned down. You've got to have a resilient ego or it gets old.

When it comes to ego, keep in mind that we're talking about the leader of the team, not the team players. The best relationship managers servicing clients are almost always directly opposite, in terms of ego, from the firm owner. Entrepreneurial-minded owners who are successful at building a business with the right scale surround themselves with people who aren't like them—i.e., people who have different skill sets. For example, the person who has the ability to go out and attract new clients is probably not the best servicing advisor for clients, while the person who's the best servicing advisor is rarely the best at landing new clients. Again, we'll cover building your team in Chapter 4.

Integrity is the sixth key attribute of high-performing advisors. Contrary to the media's negative image of financial advisors, our experience is that high-performing advisors also have high integrity.

HPFs have standardized the practice of conducting business with the utmost integrity. The attitude is "I'm going to put clients first at all costs, including me losing money." They take their role of advisor to an almost spiritual level; high-performing advisors have the kind of integrity that means doing whatever it takes to protect their clients. The advisors we'll profile in the next chapter, "The Best of the Best," *all* have incredibly high integrity. These folks would go to war for their clients.

The enormous irony to this is how financial advisors are depicted in the media. The public's attitude toward advisors is distrustful. But the reality is, these high-performing advisors would never do anything to hurt their clients. Clearly there are a few bad apples, but we have rarely found one in this group that builds to $10 million or more.

Look, we're in the business of getting yelled at. You cannot make everybody happy. Sometimes it's because of something we've done. What we teach is if we've made a mistake, we own up to it and make amends. Sometimes, however, we get yelled at when we didn't do anything wrong. The classic example is "Hey, the market dropped 20 percent yesterday." We didn't do that. The market dropped, so people's investments dropped. We can't control what the stock market does.

Our answer is simply to do what's right and follow the Golden Rule. When the market drops, we pick up the phone and call every client. If we're there until 10:00 at night, it doesn't matter; we call every single client. Relentlessly putting the client first drives everything in these HPFs.

Conviction is the seventh key attribute. This one goes along with ego. High-performing advisors *believe* in their experience; they believe without question that they are right. Every advisor out there knows that there's no such thing as a guaranteed investment other than buying a US Treasury note. There's not an advisor in the world who isn't secretly questioning the investment advice he or she gave the client.

Advisor X, for example, may recommend that you invest in mutual fund Y. He's done the research and believes that it's the right thing for you, but at the end of the day, he doesn't know that. What's different about high-performing teams is they truly believe in the investment philosophy they are recommending. They can say this for certain because most high-performing advisors have their own investments and have put their money where their mouth is. They truly believe in what they're doing because they've experienced it firsthand. The high-performing advisor says, "I've analyzed the situation, and we have seen this before, so here is what you need to do." The nonhigh-performing advisor says, "We ran the numbers and have some choices for you."

Having conviction comes from experience. Here's a story to help explain the correlation between experience and investing on high-performing teams. We have a friend named Tony who's in the construction business. He's sixty years old and has been building houses his whole career. Tony now works with his son, who's a twenty-year-old strapping buck—six-foot-two and 220 pounds with muscles everywhere.

One day, we were on the job site watching Tony and his son raise an I-beam to support a roof. They had two ladders, and they had to lift the I-beam onto their shoulders, climb the ladders, and raise it ten or twelve feet, however high the ceiling was. The I-beam weighed a quarter of a ton. We were standing back watching them lift this huge beam, could see that it was a struggle, and went to help Tony with his side, thinking the sixty-year-old could use a hand.

"Don't help me," Tony said. "Go help my son."

Sure enough, his son was struggling. He was shaking from the weight. Tony, meanwhile, had his side under control. All he was worried about was his son handling the other side. They eventually got the beam up and came down off the ladders. We asked Tony how he was so sure that he didn't need help lifting this quarter-ton I-beam at the age of sixty with a body that's starting to break down.

"Because of experience," he said. "I've lifted I-beams that size a thousand times. I know it will work, and I know I can do it. I know if I put it on my shoulder and take these steps, I can get it up there because I've done it a thousand times before. My son doesn't know that. He's twenty and has done it only a few times."

The reason high-performing advisors have so much belief and confidence in what they're doing is because, like Tony, they've been there and done that. They have their own money invested or have done this for clients many times over. That real experience is why their conviction is so strong.

Knowing yourself is the eighth key attribute. All of us perform better at different times of the day. Some advisors are not morning people. They need to have two, three, or four cups of coffee to get their day started and be organized to perform at a high level. Others perform best between 6:00 and 10:00 in the morning.

Why is it so important to know yourself and when you work best? Because you want to be meeting with clients, especially prospective clients, at those times when you're at your peak. Sometimes these meetings require you to think fast on your feet. Sometimes you need to dig deep into your base of knowledge and experience. You're best equipped to do that when you're at your high point.

If you're one of those people who crash around 4:00 in the afternoon, don't schedule a meeting at 5:00 p.m. or a client dinner at 6:00. Meet people in the middle of the day. If you're one of those people who does really well in the morning, pack all your mornings with client meetings. Advisors get limited at-bats. You want to be at your best because it takes an enormous amount of effort—thousands of dollars and countless hours—to get a prospect to come through your door.

***

Now that we've covered the most important attributes of high-performing advisors, the next chapter highlights some of the best teams we've come across in our career. We learned critical lessons from these advisors, and you will too as you determine what kind of firm you have now and decide what kind of firm you want to have in the future.

CHAPTER 3
LEARNING FROM THE BEST OF THE BEST

This book will talk a lot about finding people who have already done what you want to do and ask you to watch and learn from them. Many would call this a "mentor." We have a client who says, "A mentor is a ladder." We like that definition because it was exactly our experience. Each of the top advisors we profile in this chapter acted like a ladder for us. They taught us so much about how to get where we wanted to go and who we wanted to be along the way.

Enterprise Advisors

In a white paper, "The Purposeful Advisory Firm: Managing Your Firm By Design, Not By Default," SEI Investments divides RIAs into three categories: Startup, Emerging, and Mature. Mature firms manage between $150 million and $500 million (8 percent manage more than $500 million) and are further divided into Mature Lifestyle and Mature Enterprise firms. Granted, SEI's clients tend to be smaller than, say, a Schwab or Fidelity, but the lesson SEI is trying to teach is very real.

Advisors in the Emerging stage manage around $100 million or less and haven't yet become high-performing teams. They're at the stage where they get to decide whether they want to be a lifestyle firm or an enterprise firm. The SEI paper notes that if you don't deliberately decide what kind of firm you want to have, your firm will become a lifestyle firm by default. Becoming an enterprise firm requires establishing a serious and deliberate vision of the kind of firm you are and want to be.

Enterprise firms are run by entrepreneurial advisors. These advisors go big. They are going to scale and, ultimately, sell their business for a lot of money. These people are entrepreneurs. They have no set hours. They don't think about how many hours they work. They do what it takes and somehow balance work with other parts of their lives. Schwab's statistics on advisor working hours show that the average advisor works forty-seven hours per week, so high-performing enterprise advisors are going to be significantly above that. It goes without saying that the advisors in this chapter are entrepreneurial.

Empathy and Lifelong Learning

The best of the best advisors we profile in this chapter all have deep empathy for their clients and a commitment to lifelong learning.[7] Empathy is a classic characteristic that separates these advisors. They fight wars for their clients. They don't let bad things happen to their clients, so they take on their clients' troubles as their own.

Lifelong learning is also vital. What we knew in the 1980s and what we know today is radically different. Today you can't just go to school once; you must be constantly learning. An example of this is one of the top advisors we profile in this chapter. Lori Van Dusen's specialty was endowments and foundations, a very lucrative area. The average foundation

Today you can't just go to school once; you must be constantly learning.

7 Matt Oechsli, "Four Traits That Set Elite Advisors Apart," *Wealth Management*, May 4, 2017, http://www.wealthmanagement.com/careers/four-traits-set-elite-advisors-apart.

or endowment will have $20 million to $100 million. An advisor could make a great living with those accounts, yet Lori kept learning. She realized that the advisory world was moving to large families with a lot of wealth. With her knowledge, Lori knew that was a place she could make a big difference. She didn't just learn once and let the world pass her by—she kept learning, added to her businesses, and became even more successful.

The Best Advisors All Have a Niche

Like Lori did with endowments and foundations and later with family offices, carving out an area of expertise is something that all the top advisors have done. They are specialists, and they market themselves based around their specialty. Remember that "71 percent of teams that bring in $20 million or more in new assets have a niche."[8]

The best advisors have all carved out a niche. They each offer something unique. Having a niche allows you to build a story around your firm. When presenting to clients, that story sets you apart and allows you to create a targeted marketing plan.

Having a niche allows you to build a story around your firm. When presenting to clients, that story sets you apart and allows you to create a targeted marketing plan.

There are four steps to niche marketing. The first is to identify a niche. Below, we'll cover some of the best niches out there. The second step is to become a recognized expert in your niche. That means get a degree in it, write about it, get published, and do speaking events. For example, to become recognized experts in our niche, we gave speeches, published magazine articles, became

8 Oechsli, "Which Niches Bring the Most Riches?"

involved in organizations, and networked with business brokers, lawyers, and other centers of influence in our space. In short, we built a network so we would be near the client base we wanted to serve: business owners looking to monetize.

It's important to note *how* we got published. You may be asking, "How do *I* become published?" Well, when we did not yet have presence, and no one wanted to publish us, we bought our way in. Any advisor can do this. *Worth* and *Forbes* magazines are two examples, but there are many other media outlets that will publish articles that you write for a fee.

The third step is to develop advocates. You're looking for other professionals who recognize you as an expert and with whom you can partner to generate new business. If you're a certified divorce financial analyst (CDFA), for example, you want to partner with divorce attorneys. You want them to regard you as a knowledgeable specialist, more qualified than a generalist at Merrill Lynch. Or if you're an expert in buying and selling businesses, you would target business brokers. These are your advocates.

The fourth step is to get involved in your niche. Develop professional networks, serve in charities around your niche, and become involved in organizations that attract people who might refer clients to you. You not only want to get involved, however. You also want to raise your profile by working your way up—serving on committees and participating in speaking events and other activities that will earn recognition. Ideally, you would become president of your niche organization and add that to your résumé.

Getting involved in a peer group is essential to an entrepreneurial advisor's growth. We joined the Association of Professional Investment Consultants (APIC). As you move up, there are fewer and fewer people with more experience and success than you. These folks aren't exactly hanging around the coffee shop waiting to give you advice. They're very busy people. So you need to surround yourself with a group of industry peers. A recent Kitces podcast, for example, featured an advisor who relied on an outside group of peers to grow her practice.[9] Any group you join should always include people who are bigger than you—who have been there and done that—and represent where you want to be. APIC represented that to us.

Once you've taken these four steps, then you can really go after clients. Once your advocates and clients acknowledge your expertise, you can then use those endorsements to market yourself as a specialist.

The Best Niches

Many advisors have a surprisingly limited notion of what niches are out there and available to them. Here are some examples of the niches that generate a ton of business for an entrepreneurial advisor.

Executives

One niche is corporate executives. Even better is targeting industry-specific executives, just as advisor Mark Curtis (profiled later on) did.

This niche requires experts who can help executives deal with stock options and all the other compensation plans they receive. Understandably, they need help managing those plans. They have lots of questions: Exactly how much stock do they have and what is it worth? When should they exercise their options or liquidate? Executives with these kinds of benefits packages need to follow certain restrictions governing when they can sell, and they need tax advice on the consequences. Advising them is an expertise that few people have, so you can be a true niche marketer.

---

9 Michael Kitces, "#FASuccess Ep 075: Walking Away From RIA Partnership to Scratch Your Own Entrepreneurial Itch with Kathy Longo," June 5, 2018, podcast, http://www.kitces.com/blog/kathy-longo-ria-entrepreneurial-podcast-financial-advisor.

Business Transitions

When an owner is planning to sell their business or transition ownership, this is another lucrative niche for entrepreneurial advisors. If you're going to specialize in this area, you need to go school for it. You need to really understand how to do it because it's not just financial advisory territory; you need to be one-third CPA, one-third lawyer, and one-third financial advisor. If you're not this and don't want to become it, you need to partner with someone who is.

If you're willing to immerse yourself in learning about business transitions—or perhaps you built a business yourself and sold it—this niche is one of the most profitable ways to prospect for new business because you're getting in the middle of major financial transactions. The key is to get involved as they are thinking about monetizing their life's work and add value by helping them understand their options.

Business Owners

A specialist in helping business owners is somebody who understands the lives of business owners. You specialize in helping people who have built companies and are looking at how to monetize or transfer those assets to family or key employees. Maybe you ran your own business. If you've owned a business, you can use that experience to pursue other business owners as accounts. They have special needs around lending, marketing, and employees. The advisor who can add value here earns that business by saying, "I've been there, I've sat in your chair, and here's what you need to do." You help them investigate their options, understand the ramifications, and plan for what to do next.

Custodial Referral Program

We started in the business with a firm that grew to over $10 million in revenue by being a part of a custodial referral platform. Most custodians that gain accounts over a certain size are guided to refer them out to one of a very short list of approved RIAs. This requires you to market to those employees and advisors as the custodian, but can be very successful.

Next Generation

One of the most significant problems that ultrahigh net worth individuals have is communicating with their children about their family wealth, their values, and their mortality. If you position yourself as someone who helps affluent clients communicate with their children about key issues around how that wealth was created, how it is maintained, and how it will be transferred, you can be of enormous value to large family offices with big accounts. We became this in our family office practice. It worked to get us new clients because for most affluent folks, there is nothing more important than their kids.

Divorce

Divorce is likely one of the most difficult things a person faces in life other than losing a loved one. You can become a specialist in helping remove the financial anxiety of divorce. You help them see the other side and find peace with it so they can move forward.

A lot of money suddenly becomes available to spouses in divorces. These individuals may or may not have had to manage money in the past. Typically, they need the expertise of a niche advisor who specializes in divorce. This is another area where getting educated is important—you need to become a CDFA. These advisors provide an essential service during a trying time in their clients' lives.

Specific Company/Industry

Focusing on a specific company or industry is another niche. We see a lot of advisors become experts in dealing with physicians, who face specific issues that other people don't face (malpractice insurance being the classic example). If you specialize in helping doctors, you can provide a service to them that other financial advisors cannot by being an expert in these other areas (like malpractice insurance).

Religious or Ethnic Groups

Often people want to invest in accordance with their church's social guidelines. Mormons typically don't invest in anything related to alcohol, for example. A lot of religious groups—and their administrative bodies—also want to deal with advisors who are members of their own religion.

Specific Groups: Military and Athletes

Here you become an expert in the lives of athletes or military personnel. Career military veterans often have an enormous pension. They put in twenty years, and the pension income matches their income during their working years. Helping military families deal with pension income is one part of this niche; helping veterans plan for their second career—a common issue—is another part. It is a real niche specialty.

Athletes are a classic example as well. The average playing life for an NFL running back is two and a half years. Yet in that time, they might make several million dollars. Helping athletes—and their agents—handle that money and plan for a second career is another way to be a niche advisor.

***

The niches we like the most are the ones that hit a point in the client's life that creates a monetization event. With these events, you know that there will be money up for grabs.

Our niche came from having started five businesses, taken one public, and sold some to financial buyers and others to strategic buyers; we felt like we knew where that business owner sat. If he or she was trying to monetize his or her life's work, we knew the terrain. We knew because we had been there ourselves. We could talk to that business owner in a way other people could not because we had sat in the client's chair. We love this niche because it involves the movement of millions of dollars that people need specialists to deal with.

Another one we especially like but didn't cover above is retirement planning. Advisors who specialize in retirement help their clients understand and prepare for all the hidden costs involved with retirement. Advisors who are experts in this niche make a convincing point: "Sure, you can use financial planning software to plot out your retirement, but I have real-life experience in this. The real expenses of going into retirement aren't what any of those programs say they are."

An example these advisors will quickly note is these programs fail to show how real spending declines over time for most clients of a certain age. Those advisors will develop their niche by saying, "All those other financial advisors who don't spend time in specialty classes don't know these things. I do because of my real-life experience." Retirement is a great niche for advisors to differentiate themselves. It's also a place with a ton of assets in motion.

Some advisors become niche players by getting involved in their clients' hobbies or passions. For example, many ultrahigh net worth clients are passionate about exotic and vintage automobiles.[10] These

---

10 Mitchell Katz, "Exotic and Vintage Cars: A Passion That Can Build HNW Client Relationships," *Wealth Management*, September 27, 2018, https://www.wealthmanagement.com/high-net-worth/exotic-and-vintage-cars-passion-can-build-hnw-client-relationships.

clients have specific needs around financing and P/C insurance, as well as asset management for other funds. Normal financial advisors know nothing about this business. This was a big part of our work at our independent advisory.

With every niche, you position yourself as the solution to the problem your clients are facing. We call this "relationship alpha," which we'll discuss in detail next chapter.

The Best of the Best: Profiles of High-Performing Advisors

Why so much about niches and traits? Because you'll see them exemplified in the advisors we talk about in this chapter. They influenced our lives by being examples of what we needed to do in order to scale our practice to a much bigger level.

George Dunn

George is an industry icon. Some call him the grandfather of managed money. George is special for multiple reasons. First, he's a true niche advisor: his niche is foundations and endowments. He does have some individual clients, but when he's out talking to prospective clients and they ask what he does, he'll tell them he's a specialist in helping endowments and foundations achieve their investment objectives. He manages one of the largest asset bases of any financial advisor around.

The second thing that makes George unique is he just bleeds integrity. When you meet the man, he has a presence that is second to none we've ever seen. You not only see the credentials; you see it in everything he does and says and how he acts every day. This is the kind of guy who will go to war for his clients ahead of himself, his firm, and everybody else.

The third thing that separates George is his understanding of scaling. George became successful on his own, but then he brought in people who are now the leads on large foundation and endowment accounts. For example, he manages money for a university that hired him fifteen years ago. Today, one of George's partners takes care of that account on a day-to-day basis and George only comes in when needed. You will see in later chapters that this is critical to scaling.

George has successfully positioned his company to be monetized. He can sell the company, and the company will go on just like it does every day because he's not the guy managing the accounts. That's what scaling really is. We sought out George when we were at the wall, watched what he was doing, and learned a lot that helped us get to $10 million.

Mark Curtis

Mark is a shining example of what any advisor should want to be. He developed a very specific niche: Silicon Valley executives. These executives have stock options and other compensation that can't just sit there. It must be managed. Often, C-level executives have a lot more wealth beyond their executive compensation, so Mark is fishing in a big pond.

Mark also recognized scaling long ago. Working alone, he might have been able to handle fifty to one hundred C-level executives. Instead, he developed teams spread out all over the country—and now all over the world. He identifies the client, but then he partners with another financial consultant in that market to serve the client every day. They split the revenue. That's scaling in its broadest form. Even though this is a form of variable compensation and we believe in fixed expenses, Mark taught us so much about niche marketing and thinking outside the box. Every advisor at the wall should seek out people like this and watch what they do.

Lori Van Dusen

Lori was a specialist in the same niche as George Dunn—foundations and endowments—but she saw the world changing and altered her course. She merged her company with another company, Flynn Family Offices, and now focuses on helping family offices. Like Mark Curtis, Lori sees ahead. She's not just a niche marketer; she's smart enough to see which niches are best. She saw that helping family offices was a growing and lucrative space, and she developed a second area of expertise.

Lori also understands scaling but in a different way. She realized that when you put one and one together, you end up with three or four, not two. By merging, she gained enormous economies of scale. At the same time, she picked up great talent. Again, Lori was steps ahead of the competition here; merging separate RIAs will be another major trend in the future, which we'll discuss in later chapters.

Ron Carson

Ron used to be with LPL Financial before opening his own shop, Carson Group Holdings. What makes Ron so unique is nearly everybody else on our best of the best list is in a target-rich environment—New York, Los Angeles, or Silicon Valley. Ron Carson sits in Omaha, Nebraska.

Yet you'll find that Ron handles at least as much revenue as anybody on this list. How does he do that when he's not in a target-rich city? He understands scaling more than anybody and developed a brilliant team structure. Ron built an organization to service clients so that he would be freed up to find new business—to work *on* the business instead of *in* the business—and be the subject matter expert, which gives those clients a great deal of confidence. Now, Ron is out acquiring other advisors' practices and folding them into his infrastructure and client management system. Ron's expertise in scaling is *the* example of what it takes to get really big in our industry.

Chris Aitken

Chris was a highly successful advisor at Smith Barney. When he left, however, he unfortunately joined a company that went out of business six months or less after he arrived.

Chris lost an enormous amount of the business he had built up over the years. Why is he on this best of the best list then? Because he's the classic example of hard work, believing in yourself, then going out and executing. In only two short years, Chris took a business that was devastated and rebuilt it beyond where it was. This wasn't a small business either, and Chris received recognition as one of the Top 100 Advisors in America by Barron's. He did this by immersing himself in the communities where he was living. The execution was mouth-to-mouth, hand-to-hand, referral-to-referral, and he rebuilt a multimillion-dollar business. He's a master of referral marketing. Nobody does it better.

But you have to believe in yourself. Having gone through what he did, you must have an investment philosophy you are deeply committed to and have enormous presence. Chris bleeds presence. Every time he's in the room, people know that he's the guy who can make them a whole bunch of money.

Ric Edelman

In any given year, depending on who's doing the ranking, Ric is usually called one of the biggest financial advisors in the country. He built his one-man practice, Edelman Financial Services, into a behemoth company serving over 37,000 families with more than $22 billion AUM. Besides an incredible ability to scale, what makes Ric especially unique is how he built his business: he hosted radio and TV shows and became a recognized financial expert in the media. Ric is an impressive example of another way to build a business in today's social media world. We learned by watching him and how his unique marketing created real presence—something we found to be critical if you want to break through the wall and get to $10 million.

Elaina Spilove

Elaina started out in management. She wasn't an advisor; she was managing other advisors. Another forward thinker, Elaina recognized that management didn't give her a future in this business, and her role was not satisfying. So she got into the advisory business.

She's an example of an advisor who thrived by following the system we're talking about in this book: find advisors who are bigger than you and learn from them. She learned by literally following some of the people on this best of the best list—Dunn, Curtis, Van Dusen, and others. She followed them around, trying to figure out what they were doing. She joined APIC and surrounded herself with peers she could learn from by watching what they did.

Then she developed her own niche marketing model and put her own twist on it, which is what makes her unique and worthy of this list. Her twist was that she had some serious political connections. She could open doors in government that few others could open. Elaina became the manager of state funds in the Northeast US. Many rules are associated with managing state funds—what can be invested and what can't, reporting, etc.—and she became an expert in all those things in a space where few are qualified to do it. We learned a lot from Elaina about style and presence. She was the shining example of getting involved in niches where your marketing plan wanted you to be. But what we learned most from her was incredible grace.

***

The top advisors are all specialists. We wish we had understood earlier the need to be unique. We could have shortened a thirty-three-year journey into half that time had we become specialists in advising business owners earlier. Unfortunately, we were like every other advisor out there—just trying to knock down doors and bring in new clients one after another. We didn't have anything unique about us. We worked for big name firms, but that didn't make us unique.

The top advisors are all specialists.

It wasn't until much later in our career that we understood the importance of becoming a specialist. When we finally came to understand how important it was to specialize and we became experts in helping business owners monetize their life's work, our business exploded. We had more than $10 million in revenue by the time we sold. The key to that big expansion was understanding niche marketing and then scaling the business so we could really grow.

CHAPTER 4

BUILDING THE RIGHT TEAM

An advisor who follows everything in these pages except this chapter will eventually fail to achieve the goals laid out in this book. Failure to build the right team will result in an advisor failing to scale and struggling to have peace with his or her work-life balance. How do we know? Because we built the wrong team structure before understanding how to structure the right team. This chapter is to help you learn from our mistakes.

You must set your team up to win. Doing that means understanding what that team needs to deliver. Your team needs to serve clients in a way that differentiates you from everyone else. That starts with delivering what we call "relationship alpha": a deeper level of service to your clients.

Relationship Alpha

What's your real alpha? Portfolio alpha or relationship alpha?

"Alpha" is a word heavily used in investment management to describe asset managers who produce above benchmark returns for the risks they take in any given investment. We call this "portfolio alpha."

Relationship alpha is about creating excess satisfaction in your relationships with clients by becoming the center of their financial lives.

But there's another kind of alpha—a more important kind, we will argue. Relationship alpha is about creating excess satisfaction in your relationships with clients by becoming the center of their financial lives. In doing so, you exceed their expectations to such a level that it becomes unthinkable not to have your services. In short, you do more for clients than other advisors will or could do.

Sample Relationship Alpha Services

- Bill pay coordination
- Budgeting/balance sheet creation and updating
- P/C insurance coordination
- Health care management and consulting
- Lending management
- Estate management
- Working with children and grandchildren to help values transfer and careers develop
- Outside investment review and tracking, including real estate holdings
- Business growth consulting
- Business monetization consulting

The ability to provide relationship alpha hinges on surrounding yourself with the right team. By this point in the book, you should understand that you can't do everything yourself. As the senior advisor, there are simply not enough hours in the day for you to be CEO, COO, and CIO. You can't be the technology expert; doing lead reporting and investment research; seeing all your clients two, three, or four times per year; running the business; and leading the effort to grow it. You must have a team around you, or you'll lose the ability to scale.

We came to understand the importance of relationship alpha from real-life experience. We're not just advisors; we're also clients. As clients, we realized many years ago we didn't just want someone to help us manage our money. We wanted somebody to quarterback all our finances—not just investments but also budgeting, bill paying, P/C insurance, health insurance, and all the other things that ultrahigh net worth individuals do not want to do themselves.

A lot of people ask us, "Why don't you just do all these services for yourself?" They assume because our background is in financial advising, we do everything ourselves when it comes to our own finances. We don't. Years ago, we reached a point where attending to these functions was not how we wanted to spend our time. Instead, we outsourced. Through that experience, we realized clients are like us. They didn't want to pay bills or create budgets. Like us, they just wanted to review the work, not do it themselves.

The ultrahigh net worth investor probably owned or was an executive at a big company. He or she had a staff—a CFO to provide budgets, an accountant to pay the bills, and a benefits department to work on health care, etc. That ultrahigh net worth investor is looking for the same relationship with his financial advisor. He or she is looking for a quarterback to bring all those resources together. Fidelity's 10th Millionaire Outlook Study revealed that ultrahigh net worth clients are looking for more than investment management from their advisors.[11] They are looking for holistic services that manage their entire financial lives, bring them peace of mind, and free them from financial anxiety.

---

11 "In the Midst of the Longest Bull Market in History, Investors are Preparing for the Future—and Looking to Advisors for Help," *Fidelity Investments*, October 22, 2018, https://www.fidelity.com/bin-public/060_www_fidelity_com/documents/press-release/10th-Millionaire-Outlook-News-Release-102018.pdf.

***

There are many conversations you should be having with clients[12]—conversations no one else is having. You should be talking about the things you can do for them to make their relationship with your firm even more valuable.

You should be actively delivering relationship alpha on an ongoing basis. No clients would assume, for example, that you can take over managing budgets, bill paying, health insurance, and P/C insurance, but we've yet to meet any ultrahigh net worth clients who want to do those things themselves. They want to know the results and make the final decision but not deal with all the paperwork and time it takes to get there.

For example, it's typical for an ultrahigh net worth investor to spend over $20K a year on P/C insurance. That's a big enough number to care, of course, but you wouldn't believe the reams of paperwork you get when you have that much to insure. Ultrahigh net worth individuals are used to delegating and managing, so they want a quarterback to go through this for them and say, "I know you've got the right insurance. I had someone cross-bid it across other insurance companies, so I know you're not paying too much, and I have reviewed your list of assets and liabilities with the insurance consultant to make sure your risks are covered. Finally, I set up our annual review meeting with the insurance people so you can review all this yourself once a year and not worry about it all the other times." Another option is hiring their own insurance agent, but ultrahigh net worth individuals don't want a whole bunch of different advisors. They want one quarterback to tell them it's covered.

12 Kevin McKinley, "Seven Conversations to Have with Clients," *Wealth Management*, February 9, 2018, http://www.wealthmanagement.com/client-relations/seven-conversations-have-clients.

To drill down a little more into what it means to provide relationship alpha, your clients want the best in health care, right? But they are often confused about how to handle it. When they were working, there was a health plan; they chose from a few options and had a HR person who directed it for them. What they really want is someone to handle it for them now—an expert who can lead them to a concierge doctor, pick the right insurance plan, and manage reimbursements. Likewise, we've yet to meet an ultrahigh net worth client who wants to sit through paying bills and updating a budget every month. They want a P/L just like they had in the business that most likely created their wealth.

This doesn't mean you must do the work yourself nor does it mean you need to be an insurance agent. You can hire people (outsource) to manage the work for the client. You are the conduit to the client. When we started this process, we had no idea how powerful it was. Once we started providing these relationship alpha services, no one else knew the client's life the way we did. This made client retention soar. It also boosted referrals when we would ask the simple question, "Do you have friends who aren't getting these services?"

Recently, we got one of our clients at Lumina Consulting, where we coach FAs on how to grow their business, to adopt relationship alpha. Six months later, however, we learned that this client was not delivering any of the special services that are key to relationship alpha. Why weren't they? Nobody was calling the clients and telling them about it. This firm's relationship managers viewed these services as just more work for them, which they are, of course. Telling a client "By the way, we provide bill pay services and can handle paying your bills every month" results in one more task for the relationship manager to manage for the client. While it is more work, delivering relationship alpha is essential to growing your firm.

This means you have to manage and compensate your team based on this model. For example, you make the bonus pool based on client retention and using at least three services from the relationship alpha menu. Why? Because relationship alpha is the key to avoiding fee compression.

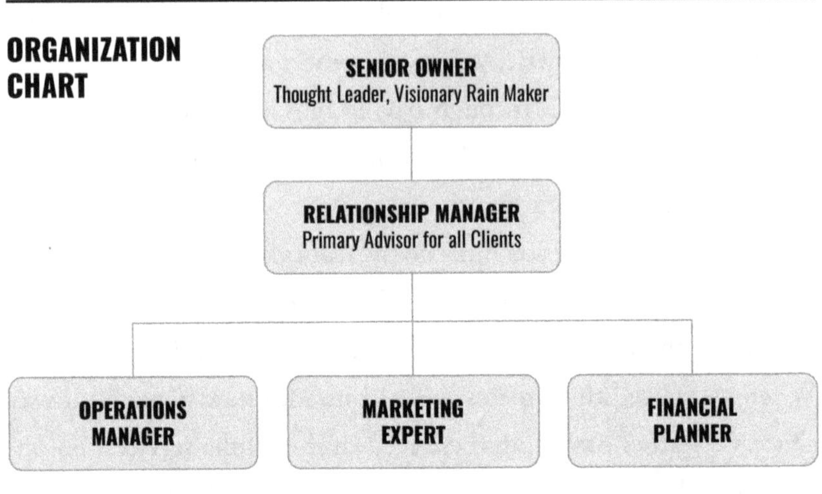

The Key Component: Relationship Managers

Schwab's RIA Benchmarking Study noted a significant percentage of firms had hired relationship managers: "In 2016, 66 percent of firms hired staff—46 percent of firms added back-office administrative staff, 24 percent brought on relationship managers, and 23 percent hired investment professionals." The study also found that a majority of the larger firms with high AUM are adding relationship managers or investment professionals at a steady clip: 60 percent of firms with \$100M-\$250M, 69 percent of firms with \$250M-\$500M, 71 percent of firms with \$500M-\$750M, 71

Relationship alpha is the key to avoiding fee compression.

percent of firms with $750M-$1B, and 96 percent of firms with over $1 billion.[13] What do these $1B firms know that you don't? They know you can't scale without relationship managers!

Some advisors may consider the term "relationship manager" belittling to their skill level or talent, but the name isn't that important—call them "senior vice presidents" if you want. The important part is the function. We like the term "relationship manager" because it speaks to the essential responsibility of this position: managing client relationships. This is the *real* financial advisor on the team. The senior advisor has become the subject matter expert; he or she needs to have an elevated position in the client's eyes. But it's the relationship manager who does the day-to-day work of watching the portfolio, rebalancing it, and managing relationship alpha services. That's why the RM is the real financial advisor. Even with institutional clients you need to employ the same idea. If there are four board meetings a year, the senior advisor shouldn't go to all of them. The relationship manager should say in one of the meetings, "I am going to ask our expert to attend our next meeting so you can hear them speak on ... "

In fact, the RM is the most vital position on your entire team. Everyone thinks the individual who created the firm is the most important person at any RIA. We disagree. The key components on any team are the relationship managers because they are responsible for delivering relationship alpha. Get this job right, and your team will do very well. Get it wrong, and your team will do very poorly.

What does a relationship manager do? He or she manages the relationships the firm has with clients. As the quarterback of the client's financial life, the relationship manager is the person leading investment meetings every quarter, setting the agenda for those meetings, managing the tasks for those clients, and looking for ways

13 "2017 RIA Benchmarking Study," *Charles Schwab*.

to deliver more relationship alpha to that client.

It's vital that those responsibilities be established in the job description for your relationship managers. As part of their bonus structure, they must have their clients enrolled in relationship alpha services like budgeting, bill paying, health care management, etc. (See the sample list of relationship alpha services earlier in this chapter.) One mistake we made was measuring relationship managers solely on whether or not clients stayed. That failed to measure whether or not they were keeping clients happy. Just because a client stayed didn't mean they would stay forever. A happy client stays forever. We learned to measure relationship managers on a different level, one that was based on whether or not they're providing the relationship alpha services that make all the difference in a client's satisfaction with your firm and therefore a client's willingness to pay current fees (read: avoid fee compression). If a client is having the RM quarterback at least three services, the odds of that client staying long term are dramatically higher.

Having an effective relationship manager doesn't eliminate senior advisors; it just means that the day-to-day contact with the client—preparing for meetings and managing all the tasks a client creates—is done by the relationship manager. The RM is coordinating all the outsourced relationship alpha services like health care, P/C insurance, and bill pay but not actually doing the work.

It's important to note here that the RM does not have to do all these things himself or herself. The RM has a team and reaches out to whichever part of the team is needed for a particular task. For instance, the RM doesn't schedule meetings. He or she makes sure that someone is scheduling four meetings with the client each year. The RM doesn't produce the investment reports but makes sure that they are ready and correct in advance of a client meeting. The RM reaches out to the senior advisor to attend client meetings whenever that expertise is needed. When it comes to relationship alpha services like bill pay, the RM hires someone and manages that for the client. Likewise, the RM isn't an expert in P/C insurance but instead hires P/C specialists and manages them.

If we had tried to quarterback the relationships for our seven hundred clients at the firm we founded, those tasks would never have gotten done. Moreover, we would have run ourselves into the ground. If we were going to scale, we had to offer these services that differentiated us, *and* we had to have somebody else managing those services for the client.

According to annual benchmarking reports, the average financial advisor/relationship manager can handle around one hundred relationships and $750K–$1 million in revenue. We think those numbers are wrong. We believe a good relationship manager can handle up to three hundred clients and around $1.5–$2 million in revenue. Therefore, for every $1.5 million in revenue your firm has, you should have one relationship manager handling that set of clients.

RMs are highly organized and have great interpersonal skills for listening and relating to others. They typically score low on marketing skills and do not desire to take large risks in their lives to get ahead. They find great job satisfaction from completing tasks and pleasing clients.

The RM is the client's one-stop shop. Every client wants to have somebody who's their primary contact and knows them. When the relationship manager already knows everything about the client, it makes the client's life that much easier and the relationship with the firm that much stronger. The client doesn't have to explain everything all the time. The relationship manager is right there in the middle, running the client's life but also working with other team members and resources to get those tasks done.

The Role of the Senior Advisor in Client Meetings

When that meeting starts, the senior advisor is present along with his or her relationship manager and the clients. The senior advisor starts the meeting by asking what's new in the client's life; updating the clients on important changes in the investment world or things that they should be attuned to in their planning; and giving them a market overview of what's going on in the economy. But then that senior advisor gets up and leaves, and the relationship manager runs the rest of the meeting, takes notes on all the to-do tasks that came from the meeting, and follows up those tasks with various staff members before the next meeting. The above scenario is just the clients for whom the senior advisor needs to be there. There are a lot of meetings where the senior advisor doesn't need to be involved at all.

Most advisors can't imagine that kind of relationship with their clients. Yet clients want to be with someone who is that much of an expert and that much in demand. If a client has $10 million to invest, would he or she want to invest that money with the advisor who sits down for every second of every meeting, who's not in demand so he or she has all the time in the world for the client? Or would the client want to invest with the advisor everyone wants to get time with to invest their money?

When the RMs quarterback the client relationships, that frees up the senior advisor to run and grow the firm. The firm owner isn't worried about whether or not a wire went out for a client by 2:30 p.m.—that's the relationship manager's role. The owner isn't worried about upcoming meetings because the team is preparing these, etc. The previously mentioned study on high-performing advisor teams notes that the bigger the independent firm, the more likely it is to have a hierarchical team structure with a lead senior advisor focused on growth and RMs managing client relationships. Fifty-seven percent of teams with more than $500 million are structured this way. For teams managing less than $500 million, the percentage with this structure is much lower—in the thirties.[14]

The role of the senior advisor is also to be a thought leader who has presence. When clients hire a firm to manage their money, the first thing they're looking for is a thought leader—an experienced, knowledgeable person leading the firm who can help them accomplish their goals. They must have confidence this exists. That means getting credentials, being published, getting ranked, and/or getting speaking engagements or quotes in the media. All this helps to build presence.

14 Kenton Shirk, "High-Performing Advisor Teams."

The owner of the firm sets the tone of what needs to be done for the client and steps in when clients have something in their life that requires additional expertise. Medical specialists have a similar role of thought leadership and modified availability. If you need brain surgery, for example, the brain surgeon is going to step in only when necessary. You wouldn't normally visit a doctor like that. Instead, a general practitioner or nurse practitioner handles routine care.

The brain surgeon is like the firm owner: the specialist who steps in when needed. The specialist provides insight when something critical is happening in the patient's or client's life. If an investment portfolio needs to be changed to protect the client, that's a place where the senior advisor steps in and provides expertise on why a change is needed. If a client has a major decision pending—such as selling a business, making an outside investment, or resolving an issue involving their children—or the market is down and they need real-life experience from someone who has faced these issues before, the senior advisor is brought in by the RM.

Our clients expected to meet with the senior advisor, but they also acknowledged that one person cannot do everything. They wanted the senior advisor focused on managing money and finding unique solutions to the issues they were facing. We wanted the client to understand that we had a team taking care of them, not an individual. And that team had a senior thought leader who could accomplish what was needed—i.e., instilling confidence. Clients want to have confidence in a senior leader who's an expert, but they want to be served by someone who has time to really serve them. They don't care about talking to the expert all the time; that's a misnomer. They just want to know the expert is there. They'd rather talk to the person they like talking to, and it's those interpersonal skills where RMs excel.

Fixed Versus Variable Costs

If you accept the notion that you need a team around you to provide relationship alpha, how are you going to pay those people? You must build your team with the right cost structure or your profitability will collapse.

One of the mistakes we made was paying people with variable costs. This is common in our industry. Financial advising is built around the old brokerage firm model: no one collects a salary, but they all get a portion of the revenue they service. This model is called "splits."

Under this model, a firm owner builds a team by bringing in other advisors and saying, for example, "Okay, I brought the account in, so I get 33 percent. You're going to take care of the account, so you get 33 percent. And then 33 percent will go toward overhead." In other words, while there are lots of versions of how to split revenue, it's variable revenue—based on what the client pays and variable costs.

The first problem with the "splits" model is that everyone has the same job function. All those other advisors you're splitting with now have the same responsibilities you have, so they run out of time, too. It's very difficult to provide relationship alpha if you're simply allocating revenue among people who have the same job function. Everyone is trying to do everything for the clients they serve, so your team is spread too thin. Providing relationship alpha requires having people dedicated to those specific efforts, people with expertise and experience working

It's very difficult to provide relationship alpha if you're simply allocating revenue among people who have the same job function.

toward every need that has to be met.

Think about if a senior advisor hires a younger advisor, and they each have the same objectives and job function. Both are trying to add clients and increase how much those clients pay every quarter. Both are trying to do a good job for those clients, service those clients, and create great financial plans. All that senior advisor has done is hire a mini version of himself. The problem is that the mini version must do all the same things the senior advisor does to build his or her business. Both will run out of time, and neither will end up providing relationship alpha. The relationship manager you hire shouldn't be trying to build their own careers just like yours. Like you, they can't be wearing all the hats. Your role is to be the thought leader and specialist whose focus is growing the firm. Their role is to provide relationship alpha.

The second problem with variable costs is profitability. When that younger advisor is being paid on a variable scale instead of a salary, he or she is getting a share of the future revenue and the terminal value of that book of business. There is no scale in that return, meaning if the senior advisor continues paying the younger advisor 33 percent of every account, that younger advisor is earning probably $300K–$500K annually to do the same work that a RM on a fixed salary of $80K could accomplish. Said another way, top performing teams bring in 60 to 70 percent in net earnings before owner's compensation (EBOC). But if one-third of revenue is paid to the younger advisor and one-third is costs, then you're making 33 percent instead of 60 to 70 percent!

Why, then, would anybody pay on a variable basis rather than fixed? Because it costs nothing up front. When the firm hires that person, there's no salary with benefits going out the door every month. It's easier to have the younger advisor handle the workload when it costs nothing up front.

Hiring a commission-based employee who will cost the firm more in the long run is shortsighted. Many owners have a difficult time investing in their own business. They simply don't want to spend the money. They have a hard time hiring employees and paying them a salary, so they build their teams with variable costs and split the revenue—then wake up ten years later to discover their profitability hasn't budged.

Remember, this book is about taking RIAs from $1 million in revenue to $5 million and from $5 million to $10 million. If you're paying on a variable basis, you will be paying much of that increased revenue to your team. Your P&L will fall apart. We have a client who hired us to find out how he could possibly be making basically the same net income after growing his firm 5X. We explained that he had variable costs and variable revenue and needed to change. How did we know this? Because we did it the wrong way until we learned this important lesson.

Don't build your team by splitting client revenue. Build your team with salaried employees dedicated to providing relationship alpha.

Defendable Investment Portfolios

Defendable investment portfolios are something we will discuss in detail in Chapter 6, but it warrants mentioning here. In our team structure, you hire people to manage client relationships so you can manage the firm and its growth. If you're going to assign RMs to manage client relationships, you don't want to send them into a war they're not prepared to fight. In other words, your investment philosophy should involve portfolios that are easy to talk about and easy to defend.

If not, the client will be confused, won't have any idea what they're investing in, and will get frustrated. If your investments are so complicated that your team cannot defend them to clients, you won't have freed yourself up at all because you'll still be going to every one of those client meetings. Relationship alpha falls apart because the investment portfolio isn't defendable, and the client can't focus on the other services.

When you build your team, it's crucial that the members understand your investment philosophy and are equipped with a defendable investment portfolio. Only then can they handle meeting with clients.

Defendable investment portfolios are also important because they're scalable. If you have set models—portfolios that all your advisors suggest to clients—then you can convincingly defend your philosophy by communicating with the RMs who will understand how to communicate with the clients.

Here's a real-life example of an investment portfolio that's defendable and scalable. When we were building out our book of business at our firm, we made an active decision to pursue clients who were at a stage in life where they most likely needed to use their financial resources to support their lifestyle rather than trying to grow for the future. In other words, we were looking for people who had already achieved—for example, people who were selling their business—instead of younger clients who were trying to grow their capital into more future wealth. This included not just individuals but institutions such as foundations and endowments that needed to pay out a portion of their funds every year.

We targeted those clients because we could use an investment strategy that we believed in and that our relationship managers could defend. We called it the "known return strategy."

The known return strategy was defined as a portfolio of stocks and bonds that all paid dividends or interest. Instead of focusing on things we couldn't control, like the S&P 500, we changed the conversation to what their investment portfolio was actually going to do. We *could* control whether the portfolio earned dividends and interest. We changed the conversation from something we couldn't control to something we could.

In other words, it didn't matter whether the market had gone up or down. We could still defend what happened in the client's portfolio in a way that made them feel comfortable. Every quarter, our relationship managers would sit down with their clients. Our quarterly meetings lasted only a few minutes (at least the investment part) when other advisors were spending hours because we could efficiently prove our investment strategy: "Here's your budget for the year. We said your portfolio would generate *x* amount of income in the form of dividends and interest to support that budget. Here's what you earned with dividends and interest this quarter, as we said you would." That's a defendable investment portfolio. If a client questioned the change in value, we would explain that the principal would go up and down, but they weren't going to spend that if they stuck to the budget.

In the investing world, the stock market goes up and down like a rollercoaster, but dividends and interest don't often go down if you do the right research. During major market drops, our quarterly client meetings were the same. We had told them that the dividend and interest income was going to come in, and it did come in. The client's income was exactly what we told them it would be. The principal may have been down, but someday that would come back. Unless the client was going to spend the principal, it didn't matter that the market was down.

Our known return strategy was scalable, too. With seven hundred clients and 70 percent of them having similar income needs, we could use the same portfolio. We didn't have to create that many models and therefore were able to scale it. It was easy for our relationship managers to understand our investment strategy, see how it would work for clients, and then go out and explain it with great confidence.

We are not suggesting this is the only defensible investment strategy. There are many. We are however saying a defensible strategy is critical to building a successful team and scaling a business. Again, Chapter 6 will go into this in more detail.

Finding the Right People

If, as a firm owner, you're going to rely so heavily on your relationship managers to manage client relationships and deliver relationship alpha, you need to consider what kind of people you should be casting in these roles. How do you ensure they can quarterback those relationships and not just come back to you to do much of the work? How do you pay them correctly so they are engaged and feel valued?

First, you've got to find the right people. Schwab's RIA Benchmarking Study notes that with 73 percent of independent firms planning to hire additional staff, "competition is likely to be keen, and firms are taking measures to attract and develop the best talent."[15]

Schwab, Fidelity, TD, and the other big custodians have their own investment divisions for clients who come directly to them. These divisions all employ financial advisors, usually called account reps, who service the custodian's individual clients.

Account reps differ from most RIA advisors in that they are paid on the salary-bonus system and are predominantly taking orders from clients. For instance, when a client wants to make an investment, he calls a Schwab account rep to ask a few questions before making the investment. The employees usually can earn extra bonus income for promoting an idea or product, so they also know how to convince clients what is best.

These account reps are tenured. Many have been working with

15 "2018 RIA Benchmarking Study," *Charles Schwab*, 2018.

clients five or ten years, so they are already well versed in the business. Believe it or not, they're working for fixed salaries of $60K–$125K. It's a classic place to recruit relationship managers.

The second place to find potential candidates are financial advisors you've met along the way—talented, smart people who are just not very good at marketing. These folks have never been able to scale or build a business. As a result, they can't generate enough top-line revenue, yet they're skilled at handling clients and understanding investments and would make excellent RMs. Every firm out there has some of these people.

Don't Hire People Like You

A word of caution about hiring relationship managers: don't hire people who are like you. If they're like you, then they won't be happy being a relationship manager—they'll want more. This is even more true if you make the mistake of paying them with variable revenue, as this attracts people like you.

We've always had a low tolerance for people who don't move as quickly as we move, which is not ideal for managing client relationships. Therefore, we would not make good RMs. In contrast, all our RMs bleed patience. We aren't the most patient guys in the world, so we looked for this quality in our RMs. Further, they are more motivated by safety (regular income, less risk in their career), and they get great satisfaction from other people's satisfaction and successfully checking off tasks that need to be completed.

Paying Your Team

Once you've found your relationship managers, how much do you pay them? One of the best sources of guidance on this is the Moss

Adams Advisor Compensation and Staffing Study,[16] which shows by job function what people are paid. You've got to be careful of coastal bias, of course, because people in New York and Los Angeles are paid more than people in Denver, but it's a great place to start. Benchmark studies by Fidelity, Schwab, TD, and Wealth & Investments (formerly IMCA) are also good resources.

When we hired people at our firm, we operated on the theory that the first two years were for us to teach the new hire and for the new hire to prove that he or she belonged at our firm. During those first two years, since we were teaching them, we didn't believe we needed to pay at the top of the market. We would focus pay around the third or fourth quartile in the study. Plus, they needed two years to show us they could add value. At the end of that period, assuming both sides were happy, then we certainly believed they deserved to be paid in the upper quartile of each of those job functions.

Typical salary ranges are below. While thinking about how you will pay your team, be very aware that "a comprehensive strategy is critical to finding and retaining key staff," according to Schwab's RIA Benchmarking Study.

- Relationship managers: $60K–$125K
- Operations managers: $70K–$100K
- Client service associates: $35K–$80K
- Investment analysts: $50K–$70K

RMs should also be considered for some type of equity eventually. Nearly all RMs get to the place where they see the owner making a lot of money and begin to ask, "Why am I not?" Future equity is a way to handle this but it is also critical you remind them that you

16 "Moss Adams Advisor Compensation and Staffing Study," *Investment News*, https://home.investmentnews.com/clickshare/selectItems.do?CSCategory=rpts9d.

took the risk. You found the clients to put the conversation in its appropriate place.

Five Rules to Managing Your Team

Most good financial advisors are not good managers. We're not psychologists, so we don't know why this is, but the personality types of a highly successful financial advisor and a good manager do not mesh. There are exceptions, but as a general statement it is true.

Therefore, it's vital that firm owners work on their management and leadership skills. Creating a high-performing team requires both. "Principals committed to growing their RIA into an enterprise firm need to recognize the difference between management and leadership," said Brent Brodeski, CEO of Savant Capital Management, one of the largest RIAs in the world. "Management is telling people what to do. Leadership is having a vision and attracting people to it."[17]

Our first rule is loyalty. Advisors who want to be successful at managing and leading their team must be incredibly loyal to those people. That doesn't mean you don't ever fire someone who's not performing. It means that what employees are looking for is the same thing clients are looking for: somebody who has their back, cares about them, and is going to help them grow in their career and in their life. It's extremely important that team members feel that way about their leader.

The second rule for managing people is making sure you set the right tone for who the company is and who you are going to be. In our case, we set a tone that we were going to do what's right for the client and we didn't care what it cost. On multiple occasions, the staff watched us write large checks for errors that they had made, not that we

---

17 Charles Paikert, "Why Building a Multibillion Dollar Firm is Not for the Faint of Heart," *Financial Planning*, October 31, 2018, https://www.financial-planning.com/news/schwab-conference-dissects-multibillion-dollar-advisory-firms.

had made. This said two things to them: one, we will do what's right; and two, we have your back. If you make too many of those mistakes, you're not going to be around, but it accomplished both those goals.

As a firm owner, because you're going to be that person for them, here's what they're going to do for you: bring you solutions, not problems. After loyalty and setting the right tone, the third rule a great leader follows is to encourage team members to provide solutions. There's nothing wrong with employees bringing problems to a manager, but they better have considered some ideas of how to solve it—not just do what you tell them to do. If someone violates this rule, send them back to their desk until they bring you solutions, not just problems.

The fourth rule is setting the standard—expecting your employees to want to overachieve and overserve the client. The best way to illustrates this is through *The Fred Factor: How Passion in Your Work and Life Can Turn the Ordinary Into the Extraordinary*, by Mark Sanborn. Fred is a mail carrier. When Mark would go out of town, Fred noticed that his mail would pile up. One day, after Mark had lived there for a few months, Fred knocked on the door. After introducing himself and finding out that Mark traveled a lot, he said, "Mr. Sanborn, can I recommend that you allow me to hold your mail when you go out of town? Or I can place your mail inside the screen door if you don't want to share your schedule with me." Mark was pleasantly surprised, in fact amazed, as he had never had such a personalized mail service.

A few weeks later, FedEx misdelivered a package to a neighbor's house that was addressed to Mark. Fred picked it up, left it in a concealed place on Mark's porch, and wrote a note: *Mr. Sanborn, Fred the Postman here. Just wanted you to know FedEx misdelivered one of your packages. I brought it to your house but didn't want to leave it in the open so you'll find it under the blanket. Thanks for letting me serve you!*

At the holidays, Mark left an envelope in the mailbox with some money and a note: *Fred, thank you for your extraordinary service. Have a great Christmas.* A week later Mark found an unusual envelope in his mail that had a stamp but was not postmarked. It was from Fred: *Mr. Sanborn, thank you for thinking of me at Christmas. I feel honored to be able to help you with your mail, and it means a lot to me that you like the work I do.*

Where does this postman come from? Really, have you ever heard of such service? Fred was not motivated by money. He was moved by a sense of accomplishment. Fred did not get his picture up at the local post office as postman of the month, get a huge bonus for this extraordinary service, or even get paid better than the other post persons. He is a government employee. So here is the question for you and your team: why does Fred do his job so well? If it was not for status, money, or promotion, what was driving him?

Sanborn calls this "The Fred Factor." The point of the story is this: how do we turn our employees into Fred Factors? If we figure that out, if we can get people to feel that way, then we're just so far ahead of the game in comparison to everybody else. How do you create a staff that works for the same reasons as Fred? Keep finding and reinforcing extraordinary service by calling out things that staff members do in a very public forum so other staff members can see it. When someone on your staff is hurting, go the extra mile to help. Make the little things big things to show you are watching and you care! Create a culture of extraordinary service, and it will become the norm instead of the exception.

The last rule is to pay people fairly (in a very transparent way, as noted above, by using the studies we talked about). If you follow these five rules, you will do well as a manager and leader.

The Power of Firing a Client

Now that you've built your team and have it up and running, what's the most powerful thing you can do to take your team to the next level?

Show them that you're on their side. One way to do this is to fire a client who needs to be fired. Staff get easily frustrated with high-maintenance clients, right? On the one hand, it's important to remind your team that high-maintenance clients pay the bills. On the other, there are times when you need to back up your staff and fire a client who's being abusive.

When you fire a client, you'll see an increase in productivity you can't even imagine. With one move, the staff realizes that you have their back. It may be one of the most powerful things you will ever do as a manager.

When do you fire a client? You don't fire a client because they're difficult because virtually all rich people are difficult. You do fire a client if they are ever remotely abusive to your staff. It doesn't matter how big the client is—they're gone.

For instance, we had a client once who was bringing in more than $80K a year of revenue. This client got abusive on the phone, not only using vulgar language but going after a specific individual on our team. We got the entire staff together in the conference room, called the client over speakerphone, and said, "You need somebody else to work for you, and we'll be happy to help you transfer your accounts." You wouldn't believe what this did for productivity. You also eliminate liability. Even though this client pays a lot of fees, they also create emotional liabilities for you and your staff. When you're not burdened by this kind of relationship, don't be surprised when things improve financially and otherwise around the office.

Preparing for the Storm

The principles we're talking about in this chapter—getting your team in place, your productivity and numbers right—need to be addressed *now* because of the lessons of 2007–2008. The message is, get your house in order before the storm.[18] Here's a great test: ask an advisor to run where he or she would be in net profits if revenue dropped 35 percent. Most advisors who had teams would lose much of their profitability, if not all.

Maybe you have too many client support staff members, or your relationship managers are handling only $700K in revenue instead of twice that. We learned this the hard way. We built a great team in the early 2000s. Our business was exploding, adding $100 million in assets under management each year. But we'd gotten ahead of ourselves. Frankly, we'd gotten lazy about the number of staff we had and what we were paying them. When people said, "I'm overwhelmed" or "I'm tapped out," we just hired more people instead of insisting that we achieve higher levels of productivity as other teams had. We simply had too many people.

In 2008, when the market declined top to bottom some 60 percent, our revenue dropped 30 percent. And we hadn't sized right—we weren't making sure our productivity was right or that our relationship managers were managing the right number of households. Our revenue dropped 30 percent while our fixed costs were the same, so we had to cut 30 percent of expenses. That meant certain staff had to go, and we lost some great people. It was a very difficult time.

But here's the shocker. In 2009–2011, we were able to go back up to higher revenue levels than we were before without adding

18 John Kador, "Six Trends in Financial Advisor Compensation," *Wealth Management*, June 27, 2018, http://www.wealthmanagement.com/industry/six-trends-financial-advisor-compensation.

back those positions that were cut. What's the lesson here? There's a problem with financial advisor structures that say relationship managers should be handling $700K in annual revenue. The industry has gotten lazy. The real number is at least twice that—RMs should be handling $1.5–2 million in annual revenue. At $1.5–2 million, you should not need more than one operations person in addition to the RM. Any staff over this is too much—meaning you are not prepared for the storm. As you grow, you can add more staff in accordance with this model, but don't get ahead of it.

Another way to prepare is to protect your client assets from a major drop in your asset management strategy or hedge your own business using options. We're always amazed RIAs don't do this. It is so easy to take action to protect your business in a drop. Other industries, like airlines and agriculture, do this every day. Expand your thought process!

A good advisor acknowledges, "There's a storm coming, and I'm going to prepare my team so we're ready to handle it." Good advisors are going to realize this now and correctly size their team before another financial crisis hits. When their staff says they are overworked, good advisors tell them, "We're not adding employees because I don't want to lose our team when the storm comes."

Managing Time

This is something we personally failed at badly. Again, this book is about teaching from failure. We believed we had to always be available to our clients, so our phones were on all the time. We never took a vacation where we weren't working. This created a lot of strains outside of us—primarily on our families.

But the other thing that our being available all the time did was create a lazy team. If your leader is always available, you never have to solve problems yourself. This was a huge revelation for us.

Since then, we've been teaching advisors about modified availability. We're now big fans of this idea for high-end financial advisors. We picked out two times every day to return calls and emails and had our staff block off those times. And we didn't do anything else in that time but return calls or emails.

We also forced our staff to set meetings on our schedules to discuss problems, which forced them to try to solve them first because they often didn't want to wait for that meeting. The way to deal with the anxiety caused by being busy is structure. Schedule everything out and have team members who can run with their job functions. That way, you can be a leader for the business and your clients. However, one point of caution: don't let a staff member or client not be able to see you or talk to you the same day they have a need.

One of the things we wish we had done is force the leading advisors in the firm to take sabbaticals. (Michael Kitces has a January 2019 podcast about taking sabbaticals.[19]) We would recommend that, every five years, these advisors need to leave the firm (no phone, email, etc.) for three months. During that time, we suggest that these advisors reflect on their five, ten, and twenty-year business plans, do some charitable work, and write about topics they care about and feel people need to know about. Whatever they do, however, the point is to get away, refocus, and emerge ready for the next five years.

19 Michael Kitces, "#FASuccess Ep 108: How to Take a Sabbatical Even When Your Clients Depend Primarily on You, with Lisa Kirchenbauer," January 22, 2019, podcast, https://www.kitces.com/blog/lisa-kirchenbauer-omega-wealth-management-sabbatical-life-planning-kinder-3-questions/.

CHAPTER 5
THE RISKS OF PARTNERSHIPS

By this point in the book, you've figured out that you can't do it all. If you want to scale, you must build a team around you to do the things you don't have time to do yourself. You now understand that the right way to build a team is through relationship managers who serve clients to the highest level and deliver relationship alpha.

For each RM in your firm to be able to handle $1.5–$2 million of revenue, he or she cannot be sending out wires and processing paperwork. So you build a team around the RM to get all the necessary tasks completed. The RM quarterbacks those tasks, and your other team members carry them out. That frees up your RMs to handle twice the revenue the benchmarking studies say they can handle.

As the senior advisor, you manage that team. But most importantly, you work on where the business is going and how you will get there. We've talked about the importance of management skills: loyalty, setting the right tone, encouraging your team to develop solutions, and paying your people fairly. A combination of having the right team in place and the right management skills is how all the successful advisors have scaled their practices to overcome the wall they're facing.

You've made the decision to change. You're ready to run a practice instead of being solely a financial advisor. There's an enormous distinction between managing a practice and just being a financial advisor, and you've recognized that this change is the only way you're going to create a business of value. Making this change is the *only* way to achieve what this book is about—selling half your practice for $20 million.

We made this change in our own thinking. Before we did that, one of the biggest hurdles we had to clear was partnerships.

Partners and Problems

Instinct tells us to go after the easiest solution to any problem. That instinct is reinforced by our industry, which has held up partnerships as the quick answer to the problem of not being able to get over the wall of $1–2 million in revenue. Standard wisdom says that combining your practice with another practice will get you over that wall. This solution sounds great in theory, but in practice it often creates more problems than it solves.

Most advisors choose to partner when they hit the wall, yet 80 percent of those partnerships are going to fail.[20] And you won't get past that wall unless you partner with someone who has enormous amounts of excess time. Simply putting together two advisors who are both hitting the wall does not allow them to scale. In fact, all it does is allow you to share your problems with somebody else.

You might ask, "Why is this the go-to solution then? Why do financial advisors do this?" They get convinced by people in our industry that if Advisor A focuses on financial planning and Advisor B focuses on investments, then putting A and B together allows you to serve clients better and create more revenue. The belief is that having your partner do half of what you were doing will give you the time to grow the business.

20 Amanda Neville, "Why Partnership is Harder Than Marriage," *Forbes*, March 1, 2013, https://www.forbes.com/sites/amandaneville/2013/03/01/why-partnership-is-harder-than-marriage/.

Reality shows this just isn't true. If an advisor is already facing a wall, then bringing on a partner to do some additional services for clients will have marginal impact on income. Adding a partner in this manner won't give the firm the capacity to become a high-performing team because it doesn't solve the problem of scalability. *Both* advisors are now hitting the wall instead of only one. Both advisors represent variable costs instead of fixed.

Partnerships fail when the partners don't have clearly defined roles. Most partnerships are set up so that one partner manages one book of clients and the other partner manages another book of clients. Each partner has the same role. We call this a horizontal team, and it's a recipe for failure.

In the last chapter, we defined what your team should look like—the relationship manager model. In that model, each role is extremely defined. The RM has a certain role, and the senior partner has another role. We call this a vertical team.

In our industry, dictatorships are better than partnerships. There must be one person leading the firm. All the high-performing advisors we profiled in Chapter 3 are alphas. They're the leaders; there's not a partner at their level. They do have partners—the RMs—but the team is vertical.

Taking on a junior partner is a step in the right direction. The senior partner runs the business and a junior partner manages client relationships. The junior partner has more capacity and isn't hitting the wall. This is just calling a RM a junior partner.

But there's often a problem with this scenario when a junior partner is brought on with a variable pay structure. If a senior advisor gives the junior partner a piece of the business, then that junior partner will continue to earn 20, 30, or 40 percent of the revenue from the clients they're serving. This is the wrong pay system if you're trying to grow because you'll be giving away a large share of revenue (or, even worse, that advisor will pick up and leave because they want their own shot at your position). There's no scalability in that setup. If you keep compensating the junior partner on a variable pay schedule, their pay keeps rising. Your economies of scale and what you make as the owner of the business are extremely diminished. In short, the junior partner eats up your profits. We've met so many advisors who are shortsighted on this; they didn't look at what giving 30 percent of their business away would mean as they continued to grow.

The senior partner–junior partner dynamic is also fraught with issues because it can create interpersonal problems down the line. Jealousy becomes an issue. Eventually, that junior partner will start questioning why the senior partner is making all the money and the junior partner is doing all the work. It must be an employer-employee relationship with acknowledgment that the junior partner's role is relationship management.

In our industry, the reality is that most partnerships fail, and the cost of that failure is much greater than you think. Having been through failed partnerships ourselves, we can tell you that it's much more difficult than just a thorn in your side. Failed partnerships take an emotional toll that will shut you down for a significant period. The breakup of a partnership is a major hurdle in your career that will cost you around a year of your life. Not that you won't make any money in that year, but you won't grow during that time. It's such an emotionally trying experience that you simply can't function at your highest level. We wish we had known this before so we would not have had to go through it.

In our industry, the reality is that most partnerships fail, and the cost of that failure is much greater than you think.

Partners and Successes

The only partnerships we see that are successful are the ones in which each partner has a specific role. While we do believe the strongest management model is a single senior partner leading the firm, you can have partners who are equal in terms of seniority but do very different things.

For example, one partner might manage investments while the other brings in new clients. Those are such different roles that it's possible for two equal partners to coexist, at least for a while. But what happens when the partner who is getting the new clients stops working as hard? The other partner has a full-time job servicing clients. It's only a matter of time until this blows up.

The best example we know of a successful partnership is a firm out of St. Louis called Buckingham Strategic Wealth. BSW built its partnership model specifically around CPAs who wanted to be in the investment management business. The company recruited CPAs—experts in taxes, of course, not in managing the financial services side of client relationships—by providing them with a back-office solution to managing client relationships.

As a result, many CPAs joined BSW because the back-end model was already built for them. This partnership was successful because the mindset of a CPA is tuned to partnership: most CPAs are salary-based and have already worked in a partnership at some point, usually for one of the big accounting firms, before deciding to start their own. The mentality of a CPA is different from a financial advisor who has worked on commission—the eat-what-you-kill model—his or her entire career.

BSW works well for three main reasons. First, it starts with people who have the mentality that makes partnerships work—i.e., having defined roles. Very few financial advisors set up their partnerships with such clearly defined roles. The second reason for BSW's success is the fact that CPAs have another job: they are CPAs first and investment advisors second, so they want someone else to handle the back-end side of the investment management. And the third reason is BSW's track record. The firm has a long list of CPAs who joined it and thrived, and that track record breeds further success.

Take these three things and combine them with a niche marketing effort (CPAs), and you have an extraordinarily successful firm.

***

Don't get lured into what looks like an easy solution to getting over the wall you're facing. There are no easy solutions. The grass is never that much greener. Instead of choosing a partnership because it looks like an easy way to grow and save a few dollars of overhead, ask what the other financial advisor does that you can't do, why it will serve the client better, how this will help you scale to the $10 million level, and why it will serve you better. If you get the right answers to those questions, then you might consider partnering. But if not, partnering is not something to pursue.

Don't get lured into what looks like an easy solution to getting over the wall you're facing. There are no easy solutions. The grass is never that much greener.

The lessons are these: first, before jumping into a partnership, remember that a high percentage fail, even those with great intentions. A partnership seems like an easy solution to a lot of problems, yet even when they're successful, they can still end badly, and you may not be willing to live with the emotional damage this causes. Finally, the only type of partnerships we recommend are vertically integrated—with an alpha leader, specified job functions, a defined marketing and growth strategy, and a defined exit plan that both partners agree to up front.

CHAPTER 6
CLEARING THE HURDLES

The last chapter covered one of the biggest hurdles to becoming highly successful in this business: partnerships. Even after we figured out the formula to getting big—becoming specialists, building a team, and scaling—there were still multiple places we made mistakes. Partnerships were one, but there were many other hurdles to clear as well. This chapter is about the other hurdles that prevent advisors from growing their practices. The first we'll discuss is asset management.

Defensible Asset Management

To our knowledge, few in our industry talk about this. People talk about investment strategies that provide alpha, or they use another technical term for outperformance in portfolios. People talk about building low-cost and tax-advantaged portfolios. People talk about alternative investments. But nobody talks about defensible asset management strategies in the context of protecting your business!

Advisors eventually get judged on the performance of our investments—regardless of how strong our marketing is, how well we service clients, or how much relationship alpha we bring to the table (although these will get you many years with a client).

You can do everything that we've talked about so far, but if you haven't built the right asset management for your firm, you won't be successful. You can have the perfect team. You can be ready to scale. You can be a manager instead of just a financial advisor. But if you haven't built a company that can successfully manage the assets your clients are entrusting you with, you will eventually fail to scale the model, which is what this book is all about.

You *must* build a defensible asset management strategy. Defensible means you can easily defend your asset management strategy with clients. If you can't, you will eventually lose clients. If you lose clients, you can't scale.

Why is a defensible asset management strategy crucial? Because no investment strategy always does well. Zero percent. No matter how you invest money, at some point you will be defending your strategy to clients. Whether you're highly skilled at managing money or not, realistically you can't be beating the index all the time, which means that regardless of your experience level, half of the time you're going to be defending your portfolio.

A defensible asset management strategy is one that can remove the anxiety of investment management from the client. More specifically, it's a strategy that can remove the anxiety of difficult markets or out of favor investments.

To remove that anxiety, you must change the conversation with clients. If you're constantly trying to get your portfolio to outperform the index—which the best money managers in the world only beat half the time—you're not likely to win that war. Is there an exception? Sure. There must be someone out there who's just an amazing asset manager and beats the market averages 90 percent of the time. We don't know anyone like that, but they probably do exist somewhere.

Assuming you're not that person, you need a different solution. We talk about changing the conversation with clients to something you can win with. What can you win with? Well, you can win by providing market-like performance with significantly less risk, for example, provided you train your client to think that way.

Something that is achievable and defendable is to build stock market-like portfolios and take less risk with them. Constantly reinforce with your clients that they will get similar returns to the stock indexes but they will take 20 or 30 percent less risk doing it. If you can demonstrate that, historically, when the market has dropped your holdings have dropped less than the market, then you have a defensible investment strategy—so long as, over time, you capture market-like returns.

Another way to change the conversation is to change it to performance you can deliver month in and month out, quarter in and quarter out, year in and year out. Our firm focused on serving larger clients who had already achieved in life. They weren't still trying to grow their money because they'd already done that. They were looking to use their money for income sources. We changed the conversation by getting them to understand that our strategy wasn't about growing their funds or competing with the stock indexes. It was about how much money their portfolio could make for them that they could, in turn, spend today.

In Chapter 4, we talked briefly about our firm's "known return" strategy. Our investment strategy was built around investing in assets that were paying dividends and interest. Instead of arguing about a portfolio's return, we talked about how much income that portfolio produced. This strategy was defensible: When clients came in for meetings to review their investment performance, we wouldn't focus on how much their portfolio went up or down—we would simply look at whether they received the income. Since dividends and interest on a diversified basis are controllable, we could control the conversation. The lesson is that it doesn't matter what your investment strategy is—adopt an investment strategy that you believe in, that you can defend, and only manage money in that easily defensible way.

Doing this means you won't be able to service every type of client. At our firm, for example, there were times when we were approached by large family offices looking for something other than income. We just weren't the right fit. Instead of changing our investment philosophy to suit their needs, we stuck with what we were good at. We didn't win every prospective client, but it's okay to lose a prospect if they don't fit within your expertise and how you're managing money. Develop an investment strategy that is defensible and stick with it! Differentiate … that's the lesson!

You're Not a Financial Advisor. You're a Business Owner

This is a significant hurdle for all owners of financial advisory businesses that are growing. Once you've gotten to the point where you've figured out the marketing, you've built the team around you with relationship managers in place, and you're starting to grow, you have a new problem. As the senior advisor, you realize you have a job function you've never had before—being a business owner.

You now manage people, a P/L, vendors, legal/compliance matters, marketing, branding, and technology, among other things—in addition to being the subject matter expert with clients. When you were a smaller advisor, these weren't job functions. Either an outside firm provided these things for you or you weren't making enough money that it was important to get this detailed. But now you've got six or ten people working for you, you're scaling quickly, and you've got to manage an infrastructure.

Being a business owner instead of a financial advisor requires a chunk of time you never had to allocate before. At this point, it's necessary to realize that you *must* allocate that time because it's going to be a big portion of what you do as the alpha of your team. Even though you're growing, if you don't adjust and allocate the time necessary to be a business owner, you'll find yourself right back against the wall.

How do successful team leaders deal with these new duties? First and foremost, they adopt the RM structure we have talked about. They also outsource many of these other functions until they get big enough to designate a partner or someone on the team to handle them. Eventually, for example, you get enough revenue to where you can hire a chief operating officer to be the business manager and oversee your vendors and P&L. But if you're an advisor hitting that wall of a $1–2 million of production, you don't yet have enough revenue to hire a COO.

Until you have enough revenue to hire someone whose focus is managing your business, you need to think through outsourcing. When you're beginning to scale, work under an outsourced model. For example, you should hire an outside bookkeeper who can produce a P&L for you every month and pay your bills. While wire house advisors have a lot of the business functions done for them, the independent shops, of course, must handle all these functions themselves.

Outsourced platform providers manage the technology you need to have, like your reporting and trading software. You want to outsource as much of the functionality as possible. Because you're trying to scale, you don't want to spend your time managing your reporting platform, trading platform, and custodian. You want to spend it delivering relationship alpha and finding new clients (scaling).

***

Platform providers come in three basic varieties. The first is the complete outsource model in which one firm handles everything. The most popular one-stop solution is a turnkey asset management program, or TAMP, which takes over all your functionality for a 10–20 percent portion of your business. TAMPs essentially use the wire house model (providing all key operational items) and implement it for independent advisors.

You want to outsource as much of the functionality as possible. Because you're trying to scale, you don't want to spend your time managing your reporting platform, trading platform, and custodian.

TAMPs base their business on volume. They charge a low fee and want to bring in as many assets as they can. A TAMP could have one hundred, one thousand, or ten thousand advisors on their platform. Advisory Group and SEI are examples of one-stop-shop platform providers that can take all functionality out of your firm. They can provide custody of your assets and do all the trading, billing, compliance, and reporting. You don't run billing; they do. They send a summary report and pay you directly. You submit trade requests, and they do all the actual trading, etc.

The second model is a hybrid where you outsource *most* functionality to one firm (i.e., you're moving to a single platform provider and using their suite of services, but you are not captive to that one provider). Orion and Tamarac use this model. They have a menu, and you choose what you want, but you don't have to use them for everything. If you choose this model, we highly recommend using the suite of services the firm provides to maximize integrations between your systems—meaning, if you choose Tamarac, use their reporting, rebalancer, and CRM. If you choose Orion reporting services, use their rebalancer and their salesforce-integrated CRM.

The biggest difference in this model is these firms are not physically doing the work for you, but they can provide software that has solutions for billing, reporting, trading, and other functions. You will need an internal staff to run these functions. The cost here isn't as high for the software as in the first scenario, where a bigger portion of your business is going to the platform provider—10–20 percent and probably closer to 20 percent—because with one-stop shops you're outsourcing *all* your functionality and need minimal staffing. In this scenario, you are moving a single provider for your platform but need staffing to manage and run it for you; otherwise you're just paying for access to the software.

The third model is one we do not recommend: you pick and choose different platforms. This is where people get lost. For example, you choose a reporting platform, like Envestnet or Orion. Then you have a separate CRM, like Junxure, as well as a separate trading platform like i-Rebal. You're managing all these platforms and trying to put them together so they can talk to each other. The pick-and-choose model means more to manage and makes scaling difficult because it takes so much time just getting the platforms to work together the way you need—not to mention the staffing to manage it all.

Cross-Check System

Whenever you have a major decision to make regarding your business, you need a cross-check system. In Chapter 3 we talked about the importance of having a peer group and what APIC meant to us. Find a peer group you trust that has people bigger and better than you. It is critical that you find a group that you know will be brutally honest with you and, at the same time, has even more experience than you.

Whether you are faced with a portfolio management decision, an organizational decision, or a client situation, the key measure is to ask, "If I get this wrong, will it affect my business in a significant way?" As business owners, we all face these decisions from time to time. Successful business owners have the ability to make difficult decisions, but it is inevitable that eventually we will be wrong. Early in our careers, we sought out advice due to a pure lack of experience. The more successful we get, the more we think, "We got this!" That mindset can come back to haunt you.

We experienced this in real life. We had had some success, and we were building portfolios with hedge funds to seek extra investment alpha. This was successful, but we were getting over-weighted in one hedge fund of funds. The HFOF success was the cause of this overweighting. We saw this and asked if it was appropriate. The fund later locked up. While investors didn't lose money, this illiquidity caused us to lose many very large accounts. In short, we were wrong!

That decision set our firm back several years. Reflecting on this years later, we asked what we should have done differently. We had come to the decision with the advice of our partner, a very successful advisor and businessman in his own right. In other words, we had sought confirmation yet still got it wrong. What we missed was getting *outside* confirmation. We failed to get the input of someone who had no skin the game—someone whose emotions were not tainted by being in the business every day.

You must cross-check with advisors you respect who can look objectively at the problem and tell you if you're wrong. *Always* seek outside confirmation on major decisions. That's why having a peer group is so critical.

Smart Growth Means Maintaining Price Integrity

Financial advisors tend to take on accounts based on whatever price is required to get the account. This was a mistake we made, and we continue to see this mistake being made today by firms we consult with.

Financial advisors have a "grow, grow, grow" mindset. If we see a big account that we can get at half the price we use for other clients, we go for it. This comes back to haunt us. If you don't maintain price integrity, your profit margins will continue to drip away as your relationship managers reach capacity. You'll keep your RMs busy, but one RM will be making the company a lot more money than another, through no fault of their own. It'll be your fault for having taken on business at the wrong pricing, and, at the end of the day, you will have grown for nothing because your net income will see only small improvements. Earlier we told you that the best practices that are growing bring 60–70 percent to the bottom line before owner's compensation. When we see a really good firm at 50–55 percent, we often find that not maintaining price integrity is the reason why.

Growing for growth's sake is a common mistake. It causes advisors to discount their pricing to attract new business. We don't believe in this practice. Instead of lowering your prices, focus on providing value to your clients and maintaining your pricing. Otherwise, your ability to reach your end goal—selling half your business for $20 million—will be at risk. When your pricing is too low, your margins are too low to do what this book is about.

Instead of lowering your prices, focus on providing value to your clients and maintaining your pricing.

Instead of discounting, have the fortitude to believe in who you are and the value you provide. We learned this lesson from Frank Campanale, who ran E.F. Hutton/Smith Barney's Consulting Group. Frank would always repeat one of our favorite lines of all time: "Price is only an issue in the absence of value."

Example of Discounting

An RM with an average account size of $1 million has 150 accounts at 1 percent to manage. RM cost is $100K a year, so gross profit is $1.4 million before COS. If your other costs are 40 percent of sales or $600K, your net income on this RM's book is $800K or 53 percent net margin, which is average after RM cost, as you grow, costs will come down, increasing this net. Owner now decides to discount half of those accounts to .75 percent. Now revenue is $1.31 million, and your profit is down to $1.21 million. Take the same $600K of costs, and now you're down to $610K on this RM's book, which is a 40 percent net manager. This is way below average, caused by discounting.

Burnout

Any advisor who's been in this business awhile eventually experiences burnout. This is another significant hurdle that must be planned for and overcome. We *all* go through burnout at some point, especially those who've been in the business for twenty years or more.

Burnout comes when you have been at it for so long and you feel like you've given up so much to build the business. You've sacrificed time with your family and your hobbies. You're tired. You don't know what you're going to do, but you know that you're tired. You're starting to think about exits or moving back to the lifestyle advisor model.

How do you deal with getting tired and burning out? We touched on this early in the book, but it bears repeating. First and foremost, you must have a belief system—faith or something like it. Your belief system is your backbone for dealing with the stress this business inevitably causes. Second, you take impeccable care of your body and health. And third, you make sure to have a long-term plan so you know where you are headed and can therefore see the end of the tunnel.

Why a long-term plan? It's energizing for an advisor to know where he or she is going to end up in the future. Many advisors nearing burnout can't see the light at the end of the tunnel. It's exhausting to keep working day in and day out without knowing what lies ahead. Having that long-term master plan in place shows you that if you do *this*, *this*, and *this*, you'll be able to sell your business for *x* amount and monetize your life's work. As soon as you know that, you no longer feel burned out because you can see an end.

Advisors facing burnout need to go back to their plan and reread it. They need to talk to other advisors who have been there, but they also need to take time away to refocus and reenergize. One of the things we would have done differently is follow the CPA model and force senior people to take sabbaticals every five years, as we covered in Chapter 4. In a real sabbatical, the individual is truly cut off from the business. No emails or phone calls. He or she is encouraged to do something that allows that person to grow—whether it's a charitable cause, an academic pursuit, or simply reading. This practice of forced sabbaticals would have saved many friends in the industry we watched burn out.

False Profits

There's an old saying in our industry: "Don't get married to an asset manager." We coach advisors who want to grow to find role models among peers in the industry who are bigger than them. But in our zeal to find high-performing peers to learn from, sometimes we get attached to one individual. This is another challenging hurdle.

We made this mistake early in our career. We became attached to one individual—the extraordinarily successful hedge fund manager we talked about earlier in the chapter. The golden cup seemed to follow this guy around, so we tried to replicate what he was doing and got comfortable just following this one individual. That's dangerous. If you get too comfortable following one person and his or her ideas, you stray from your own beliefs in asset management. You say, "Hey, there really are people out there who invest money better than everyone else. This guy has the track record to support that." You start tilting your portfolios and philosophy too much in that person's direction, which is exactly what we did.

Eventually something went wrong at the hedge fund manager's firm. His investment fund locked up, and investors couldn't get their money out for a short time. Nobody lost any money, but it cost us clients who left because that fund was temporarily inaccessible to them.

When you fall in love with an asset manager or a peer and take a shortcut by following their example—instead of following your own process—bad things usually happen. Don't get married to an asset manager, a stock, or an investment fund. This is a rule every advisor should respect. As noted earlier, have a peer review your portfolios so you can have a fresh set of eyes making sure you're not missing a critical error.

Process, Not Product

Along the same lines, another hurdle is falling in love with selling a product instead of following a process. Many advisors fall prey to this, especially in the middle stages of our careers when we're trying to figure out how to get to the high-performing level. Instead of going through the process of sound financial planning and sound investment management selection, we rely on a product that's easy to talk about with prospective clients.

The hurdle here is to make sure you don't take shortcuts. You must employ a process in your practice that is not only sound but also implemented consistently. The difference between a process and a product is how you got to what you're recommending to clients. Did you employ a written process to search for the right solution? Or did you have something in a box that you just used for most clients?

This comes down to how you implement financial planning and investment management. On the financial planning side, we often take shortcuts when we meet a new client who comes in, see that it's obvious what they need, and then we go and fill that need—instead of going through the many-hours-long process of building a formal financial plan.

For example, we get a client who has just retired and needs $10K per month to retire on. We go through his asset list and see that he has $10 million. We say, "Okay, this is easy. We'll just take that $10 million, invest it in an income portfolio paying 4 percent, which will yield $400K, and after taxes we'll have excess capital to yield that $10K monthly." You know your client needs income to replace the money he was earning before he retired, so you use a mutual fund that provides that much income. You fell in love with that mutual fund and its track record, so you just repurpose that solution to satisfy the client's need for monthly income.

That's taking a shortcut that could cost the client down the line. You haven't taken the trouble to thoroughly consider all the angles. Product people have jobs; process people have careers. An advisor who's building a career should review all the client's assets and liabilities. During that process, you might discover the client has liabilities or will have significant draw-down needs in the future—maybe it's college debt that still needs to be paid off, the expense of a disabled child who needs care, or a looming major life event.

The hurdle is taking shortcuts in the financial planning process because you think you've got the automatic solution. You really like the solution, and you know the client will, too, because it's exciting and easy to explain.

Yet, down the line, you may encounter problems with that solution. In the rush of your day-to-day activities, you've skipped some steps. You forgot to ask the right questions. This could come back to haunt you when things come up that you didn't anticipate and the client is unhappy his or her portfolio, as well they should be, because the performance of that fund that was so good for so long suddenly isn't.

It's also vital that you employ a process on the investment management side. We are not trying to promote any one investment management theory. There are many different investment management theories that work, and we don't believe that any one is necessarily better than any other one. But we do believe that an enormous number of financial advisors get focused on a product as a solution, instead of following a process.

Your firm needs a process for considering every available solution—every available asset manager—and determining the right one for each client.

The best advisors search all the potential asset managers. They look at statistical measures of those portfolio managers, such as the max draw-down that each has taken. They ask questions: What's the correlation between the different investment styles? What's the effect of rising interest rates on this investment? What's the effect of a big market falloff? In short, they try to simulate what that portfolio will do in the best, worst, and expected outcomes so that the client is fully prepared.

Again, we are not suggesting that there is one investment management theory you must follow. We are saying that the best practices we've seen all follow a disciplined investment strategy to find the right solution for every client. Having a disciplined, consistent strategy also allows a firm to have an extremely well-thought-out answer to the question of how they chose each investment they recommend. They can visibly show a prospect or client why they chose Investment A over B, C, or D.

Here's a good test. Go sit down with an advisor who does twice the revenue you do and has been in the business twice as long. Present your investment management theory and see if that advisor would buy what you're recommending or if he or she sees holes in it. If that advisor won't buy it, go back to the drawing board.

In addition to your own investment management strategy, we also advocate investing in things you personally believe in and that affect your daily life. In other words, have some passion for what you invest in. Our favorite advisor who does this developed a growth portfolio made up of stocks that she believes affect her life and her clients' lives every day. Her pitch about how she got to this portfolio is sound: she talks about how when smartphones were first invented they radically changed her life—how having this thing we carry around all the time was such a significant factor in being able to organize her life and make her more productive. She saw that the value of companies responsible for smartphone technologies was going to rise, so she invested in them.

Of course, we're not saying you should invest in smartphones. We don't care what investment philosophy you come up with as long as you're passionate about it. Another example is several of the advisors profiled in this book who passionately believe that they source better investment opportunities than most advisors. They speak about access to strategies most people can't get and why that differentiates them.

A final example is another of our favorite advisors who uses a study by Dr. Marston (Wharton School of Business) that shows the number of listed companies has shrunk dramatically over the last several decades—concluding that there is less opportunity to outperform in publicly listed equities. He then pitches private equity and its track record as the difference maker. If you want a career in this business, you've got to have ideas that make you different. If nothing about your investment management is unique, and if you can't show passion for it, then you're going to have a hard time differentiating yourself. If you can't defend it, you will eventually lose.

Another example is how we invested money at our firm. We were tired of constantly being measured against the S&P 500 or another static index that the best managers in the world only beat 50 percent of the time. So, as discussed earlier, we changed the narrative to something we could control and that we believed in and had passion about. We knew we could earn dividend income and could measure performance in client portfolios by whether or not they earned that income. We believed in this because we invested in this strategy ourselves. We talked about it with a great deal of passion because we had been there, done that, and knew we could deliver.

Don't Let Yourself Become a Victim

Bad things will happen in your career. They happened to us, and they will happen to you. The question is not *if* they will happen, but what you will do *when* they happen.

It is so easy to become "the victim." This person caused this, or these people are just jealous, or this guy took advantage of me, or that person was just lucky, etc. Our real-life experience is that good things come to people who work the hardest, have the purest hearts, and don't make excuses. If you're not getting ahead, don't say other people are lucky or born with a golden spoon. Instead, figure out how to get what *you* want.

Bad things will happen in your career. They happened to us, and they will happen to you. The question is not *if* they will happen, but what you will do *when* they happen.

Life is hard! People get sick, people die, people who are not as nice as you are getting ahead. How will you respond? Will you be a victim and complain the rest of your life about how the world shafted you? Or will you get back up and fight even harder than you did before, harder than you even knew you could fight, to not be that victim?

We are in a performance-based, high-pressure business. Someone is always upset, someone always has bad things happening, and someone always has it easier than we do. When this happens to you and you are mentally exhausted at how unfair it is, follow these steps:

1. Get away from where the bad things are happening for a day or two at least. If the bad things are happening at work, take time off—not weeks, but enough time to reset.

2. When you are away, go find peace. We talk a lot about our faith as the place we find peace, but whatever yours is (music, workouts, etc.), get back to neutral so you can look at the problem with a fresh face.

3. After completing Steps 1 and 2, then and only then call someone

smarter than you—someone who has been in the business and is where you want to go. Then call another one. Ask them what they would do or, more likely, what they did do.

4. Become an inspiration to others rather than a victim. If you're sick and it feels unfair, find out how to still achieve what you want and deal with your sickness. Make the illness you are facing the niche in your business that allows you to relate to clients better than anyone else.
5. Realize this is an important time and the decisions you make now will chart a course for the next several years. Take the time to do it right. Realize also that you are not the only one who has been here. We all were!

Do What's Right, and the Rest Will Work Out

We end this chapter with a guiding principle that will help you clear every hurdle we've talked about thus far: always do what's right for the client. Defend the client at all costs. If you write that on the mirror you look at every morning and you truly live by those words, you won't take any of the shortcuts we warned against in this chapter. If you judge everything solely by the standard of what's best for the client, the rest will work out. It's the Golden Rule: do unto others as you would have them do unto you! (Luke 6:31)

CHAPTER 7

RUNNING YOUR PRACTICE LIKE A BUSINESS

There are ten key steps to running your practice like a business:

1. Write your value statement and vision statement.
2. Develop one-year, three-year, ten-year, and twenty-year plans.
3. Track business monthly, compare it to peer groups, and make course corrections.
4. Understand the tax advantages.
5. Set your prices and stand by them.
6. Plan for capital expenditures to keep growing.
7. Plan for 2008: what you'll do if the market falls by 40–60 percent.
8. Have a philosophy regarding paying your team.
9. Remember that replacing difficult employees or vendors may result in new problems.
10. Schedule meetings with your family to plan and set goals—just as you do with your business.

Write Your Value Statement and Vision Statement

The advisor we keep talking about is hitting a wall. He or she is doing $1–2 million of revenue but has not been able to grow beyond that. He or she is trying to figure out what to do next. When we were at that level, we kept asking, "What should we change?" There just weren't enough hours in the day to grow any further. We couldn't figure out the solution, so we just kept asking that same question.

Then we realized that instead of asking "What should we change?" we needed to be asking a completely different question: "What's the value we're going to offer clients?" Understanding that *providing value* to clients was how we would grow allowed us to break through the wall we were facing. Your value statement sums up the value you're offering clients. Schwab's RIA Benchmarking Study stresses the importance of a sound value proposition to high-achieving firms: "Delivering a differentiated value proposition based on the wants and needs of ideal clients helps firms earn and retain business. Firms that have documented their ideal client persona and value proposition earn 26 percent more new clients and 41 percent more assets from them than those without these strategies."

You must understand what your value is to the client and build a service around that value.

To get over the wall, you must understand what your value is to the client and build a service around that value. We realized that we needed to be the quarterback of our clients' lives and develop the list of services we talked about in Chapter 4. We understood the real value we provided was relationship alpha, not investment alpha. "Firms thrive when focusing on the client experience," reads Schwab's study.

Once we started to build our practice around relationship alpha, it became clear that we needed a team. Everything else grew from there. Step one is to know your value, and step two is to create a vision for where you want your firm to be in the future.

The value you provide depends on your niche. At our firm, we quarterbacked family offices. Other firms have different niches. Decide on your niche and then figure out what the value statement is going to be for those clients. What value are you going to provide the set of clients you're going after? Remember that value should be unique and easily sets you apart from other advisors. Simply saying, "We do great financial planning" is not a unique value statement.

Everyone reading this book needs to go away for a long weekend, turn everything off, sit down with a pencil and paper, and start to write. You must create a value statement articulating what you offer clients, what makes you different from other advisors as a result of this, and how you will offer these things that make you unique. Then you create vision statements expressing where you want to be in one year, three years, ten years, and twenty years.

Develop One, Three, Ten, and Twenty-Year Plans

Your company should have a vision statement on each of these time increments: one year, three years, ten years, and twenty years. Again, Schwab's study noted the importance of strategic planning to independent firms' success: "Most well-managed RIAs that engage in strategic planning are better able to achieve their growth goals in retaining and gaining clients."

In the one-year time frame, the vision does not need to go into how much revenue or how many clients you're going to have. It needs to talk about how you're going to change the practice to deliver value to your clients. How are you going to reorient everything you do around that value?

This vision also needs to have a marketing plan detailing how you are going to go after that set of clients. In year one, that marketing plan may be differentiating yourself by getting accredited, getting the right education, getting involved in organizations, giving speeches, or writing a book. Finally, the one-year vision needs to articulate how you will keep your existing clients and serve them with this new value-oriented model.

The three-year goal should have clear numbers attached to it: the number of net new clients you're going to add and the number of clients you're going to get rid of because they don't meet your vision. The plan for this time frame should also state the team structure (with job descriptions) that should be in place by that three-year mark. The plan must account for attrition and detail how you will go after new clients and how you will allocate time to focus on this through the RM structure.

The ten-year goal is the maturity goal. Your ship is now well across the ocean. At this point, you should be able to measure how far you are toward your twenty-year goal of monetization. If you want to walk away with $20 million for half your business, you know that you need around $1 billion in assets under management. So the ten-year mark is a check-in where you're saying, "Okay, we turned the ship, we've got the right people in the right places, we've been adding the clients that meet our value statement and vision statement, and we've become a niche player where we're an expert in our space."

"Now, where do we stand toward achieving our ultimate monetization goal? Is it realistic?" That's the key word. Is it *realistic* that we'll make it within the twenty-year time frame? Can we add and manage this many clients? Within the ten-year period, most advisors go through a period of purge—where they give away smaller accounts and take a step backward in order to take a step forward. The advisors who will achieve the level of scaling we are describing do this a different way because they have realized the power of fixed costs and the RM model. That's usually when they bring on additional people to manage the client relationships.

Remember that good relationship managers can handle $1.5–2 million of revenue. (When we started, $1 million in revenue handled by an advisor was elite; now it's average.) If your firm's $1 million in revenue comes out of a 1 percent fee, that means you have $100 million in assets under management. To manage $1 billion in assets, you'll need between five and ten relationship managers. We had five at our firm.

The point is to work backward to your goal. If you need $1 billion in assets and the average account size is $1 million, you will need one thousand accounts to produce $10 million in revenue. To service $10 million in revenue, you need around six RMs.

Track Your Business Monthly and Make Course Corrections

You must be tracking your business monthly and constantly comparing it against a peer group to see where you stand. The monthly tracking should have a P/L, and net income should be listed in the form of earnings before owner's compensation, or EBOC.

You should be tracking net new households, assets under management, and revenue by employee, among other markers. You should then be comparing those numbers to other organizations of similar size. Use the benchmarking studies from Schwab, Fidelity, and TD. They show what you need to track and how you're faring compared to other RIAs. All categories should be tracked versus other practices of your size and, in particular, what kind of numbers the high-performing advisors are doing in each of those data sets.

What if your peer group is doing better than you? Then it's time for course corrections. The whole point of tracking is to allow you to zero in on your strengths and weaknesses. If your weakness is that you're not adding the number of net new households that your peer group is adding, start to focus on marketing (using the ideas from Chapter 8, "How to Grow Your Business")—highlighting *your* expertise in *your* niche—to get more clients coming through the door.

If you're not getting the same percentage of EBOC—high-performing teams are around 60 percent—you likely have an economics problem. Either you are spending too much on overhead or are not charging enough for your services. In such cases, nine times out of ten, we find that firms aren't charging enough for their services. As discussed earlier, many advisors lose price integrity. If your EBOC is not where it should be compared to your peer group, you're probably not charging the same percentage on assets, which you can get from one of the benchmarking studies. If your revenue per employee is not on par with your peer group, you have too many people. Overhead and pricing problems are both correctable. The solution is sometimes hard to see, however, when you're smack in the middle of the business. If you're overstaffed, obviously you have to let some people go, but you also have to solve the problem of not adding enough net new households that are right kind of client. You have to better define your niche and improve your marketing toward that set of clients while reducing expenses. The next chapter, "How to Grow Your Practice," covers marketing.

Shockingly, we went through two fee increases at our firm without losing a single client. We thought we were going to, yet we learned that if we were providing great value to our clients, price wasn't an issue. We mentioned Frank Campanale last chapter, and his words are worth repeating here: "Price is only an issue in the absence of value."

We increased our prices by 10 percent each time without losing any business because we were providing great value to clients. Now, we did have a few clients who were hesitant about paying the new fee, so we came up with a compromise: "Okay, we'll do a discounted fee for a year. If we prove ourselves, then you'll move up to the normal fee." Within that next year, almost every client agreed to pay the increased fee. Why? Because we were the quarterback of their financial lives. If you're reading this and saying, "I can't do this," then there is something wrong with your value statement.

If you think you can't increase prices without losing clients, and your current prices are 1 percent or below, you're wrong. You can. But only if you're providing great value to those clients.

Understand the Tax Advantages

One of the biggest surprises when we started our own firm was the ability to materially affect how much we paid, as partners in that firm, to the IRS. We knew a huge advantage would come when we decided to monetize and sell—as we would get capital gains treatment and have a cost basis in the value of the asset we were selling. We just didn't expect there to be other benefits while we still owned the business.

As an RIA owner, you have advantages over working for someone else, whether it be a wire house or an independent firm. If you work for someone else, you're taxed for ordinary income. Further, with the new Trump tax law, when working for someone else, your ability to deduct business expenses has been severely curtailed. One of the surprises we are seeing is state-based revenue services going after wire house advisors who do business in other states than where they reside.

If you own your own RIA, only a small portion of your income will be taxed as ordinary income (provided you have a good counsel), and the rest can qualify for treatment at 20 percent plus the Obamacare tax (3.2 percent for most) and your state tax. Further, most of your expenses can be netted against gross income to produce lower income. You can also create a true cost basis in the asset you will eventually be selling by following what you paid to set up the company, capital infusions, and add on capital for things like acquisitions. This all adds up to a significant spread in after-tax income.

However, this pales in comparison to the tax advantage when you sell the asset. Again, if you work for someone, especially with today's enhanced retirement programs, you can retire and get paid over a series of years—but there is a significant chance those payments will be taxed as ordinary income. The bottom line is when you own your business and sell it, you qualify for capital gains rates, which could mean as much as a 23-point spread. If you're going to receive $20 million, the tax spread could result in $4–6 million more for the advisor who owns their own business.

Discounting is the Death of Profitability

TEAM REVENUE					
Year	**New HH's**	**Average Account Size**	**Team Growth (AUM)**	**New Revenue (1% of AUM)**	**Team Reoccuring Revenue**
1	10	$750,000	$7,500,000	$75,000	$1,000,000
2	10	$750,000	$7,500,000	$75,000	$1,075,000
3	10	$750,000	$7,500,000	$75,000	$1,150,000
4	10	$750,000	$7,500,000	$75,000	$1,225,000
5	10	$750,000	$7,500,000	$75,000	$1,300,000
6	10	$750,000	$7,500,000	$75,000	$1,375,000
7	10	$750,000	$7,500,000	$75,000	$1,450,000
8	10	$750,000	$7,500,000	$75,000	$1,525,000
9	10	$750,000	$7,500,000	$75,000	$1,600,000
Totals	**90**	**$6,750,000**	**$67,500,000**	**$675,000**	**$12,375,000**

TEAM REVENUE WITH DISCOUNTING					
Year	**New HH's**	**Average Account Size**	**Team Growth (AUM)**	**New Revenue (.75% of AUM)**	**Team Reoccuring Revenue**
1	10	$750,000	$7,500,000	$56,250	$1,000,000
2	10	$750,000	$7,500,000	$56,250	$1,056,250
3	10	$750,000	$7,500,000	$56,250	$1,112,500
4	10	$750,000	$7,500,000	$56,250	$1,168,750
5	10	$750,000	$7,500,000	$56,250	$1,225,000
6	10	$750,000	$7,500,000	$56,250	$1,281,250
7	10	$750,000	$7,500,000	$56,250	$1,337,500
8	10	$750,000	$7,500,000	$56,250	$1,393,750
9	10	$750,000	$7,500,000	$56,250	$1,450,000
Totals	**90**	**$6,750,000**	**$67,500,000**	**$506,250**	**$11,531,250**

Looking at the chart, we begin by assuming a firm is starting with $1 million of revenue. They close ten new households a year with an average account of $750K, so total new assets a year is $7.5 million. If we assume the average fee is 1 percent, revenue would increase by $75K a year. Over ten years (with the first year's growth being counted in year two), we would increase our recurring revenues by $675K a year and add ninety new households to the business. Our total accumulated earnings over ten years would be $12.375 million.

By discounting 25 percent (moving from a 1 percent average fee on AUM to a .75 percent average fee), with the same number of clients and same average AUM we would reduce our annual earnings from $675K to $506,250 (or, essentially, the cost of a RM to manage that new business). In addition, accumulated earnings over that same ten-year timeframe would decrease by over $800K—while managing the same number of clients and having the same workload!

This chapter is about running your practice like a business, which means it's about profits. It's great to win new business, and it sucks to lose a prospective client because a competitor prices below you, but the problem is not the price. The problem is that you didn't show the prospect that you offered them enough value. That was a harsh lesson for us to learn.

We would go into closing meetings for a $20 million account. We had that account priced at forty basis points, or $80K a year, but then another firm came in and did it for $50K a year. We'd say to ourselves, "Well, that's just because they're pricing cheaply." We were wrong; that wasn't why. We weren't providing enough value to the client. We hadn't yet become niche players who truly believed in our expertise and could easily distinguish ourselves from competitors.

A real-life example came in our fifth year. We were doing really well and had just been recognized both by the company we worked for at the time and the *Denver Post*, where a story about us ran on the front page of the business section. We came to a closing meeting filled with confidence. Our plan was solid. The investments we were proposing had a great record. We thought we were good to go.

But we ended up losing the business. We blamed our pricing. Later, we met the prospect again and had the opportunity to ask why he didn't choose us. He responded that he was looking for a specialist in family offices who helped people like himself. We asked if it had anything to do with pricing—surely, we thought, the advisor he chose would have been charging significantly below what we were charging.

We were completely wrong. That advisor was actually charging *more*. We were shocked. The prospect went on to tell us that, in his life, the $30K difference in fees didn't matter nearly as much as making sure someone could handle the things that he needed to get done. He wanted an expert! It was at this point that we really came to understand the importance of specializing, providing relationship alpha, and being the financial quarterback. Once we checked those boxes, we could charge a premium for our services with the confidence that we were providing clients rock-solid value.

Discounting shows a lack of conviction. One of the best of the best advisors we profiled in Chapter 3 says that the reason advisors discount their services is because they don't believe in what they're doing. Once we became specialists in family offices, helping people who were selling their businesses, and we learned to provide relationship alpha by quarterbacking our clients' financial lives, we rarely lost another deal. We provided so much more value than anyone else that price wasn't an issue. Prospects still asked, "Why do you charge this much when Company X charges less?"

We'd explain why: "Because we're specialists in this area."

Early on at our firm, a lot of meetings with prospects were about investment management and how we were going to manage their money. As we came to learn the importance of providing value, those meetings shifted to discussing all the additional services we provided. Prospects cared about the relationship alpha we were offering them, and a lot less time was spent on investment management.

If you're saying, "Clients want investments that make them money, not this relationship alpha crap," we were just like you. But then we started looking at client surveys and were shocked to see that investment performance is not the most important thing to clients. In fact, it's not even second or third.

When we became clients ourselves, that was when we really understood. We had achieved some success and had resources we needed help managing. We knew *how* to do all the relationship alpha services—budgeting, bill pay, P/C risk management, and health care planning—we just didn't *want* to spend the time doing it ourselves. Now, we wanted a financial quarterback to stand next to us and coordinate all these services. If we thought two firms could offer similar investment performance, we were definitely hiring the one that could quarterback all these services.

Now, we're not saying that clients with $500K in assets think this way. But we are saying that clients with $10 million to $50 million in assets *do* think this way. You can win by providing relationship alpha to those ultrahigh net worth clients.

Planning for Capital Expenditures

There is no successful business in the world that does not account for CapEx, or capital expenditures. The same must hold true for your financial advisory business as well—budgeting a line item for money you're going to spend to retain current clients and keep growing. You need to budget for technological improvements, for example, including new software that makes jobs easier and productivity higher and allows you to be cutting edge in what you're showing clients. You need to put CapEx in for adding people at various levels as you grow. You also need to put CapEx in for taking care of your people, which means budgeting for appropriate salary increases.

Each of your plans identified above—one year, three years, ten years, and twenty years—needs to include thoughts about capital expenditures. For example, you should be able to predict when you'll need additional RMs and customer support people and when to start looking for these people, following the metrics we provide in Chapter 4, "Building the Right Team." Likewise, you must have someone who is always looking to improve your platform and is investigating different technologies to increase productivity.

Accruing $50K a year for CapEx is a good starting place. But having a person dedicated to this task is essential, or you need to outsource this and have someone else do it for you.

Planning for 2008

You need to have a worst-case plan—what you're going to do if the market falls by 40–60 percent, as it did in 2007–08. This kind of event would impact your income by a similar percentage, of course, because fee-based businesses in our industry are heavily tied to what the market does. What do you do to make sure that your business not only survives but remains profitable? What do you do to ensure that you can continue to provide your clients the level of value articulated in your value statement?

When your income has fallen and you need to cut expenses, unloading a few people from your team looks like an easy solution. But letting go of a few staff members won't be enough to weather the storm of a market crash. Let's say you're bringing in $1.5 million in revenue when the market falls 50 percent. Now your revenue drops to $750K. When you had $1.5 million in revenue, you would have had 60 percent EBOC profitability if you were high performing, or 30–35 percent profitability if you were low performing. After the market crash, a firm that had 30–35 percent profitability is now losing money because that firm still has around $1 million in expenses and only $750K in revenue.

The number-one strategy to protect your business is to plan for it in advance by properly structuring your employee compensation. As covered in Chapter 4, you put everyone on fixed salaries rather than a variable cost pay structure. You make sure that your major expense item—which is always people in this business—is set up so you can scale the bonus side of their compensation, not the salary.

Fixed cost doesn't mean you must hand out large salaries. You can have smaller salaries with larger bonuses based upon the performance of the entire organization. A relationship manager, for example, may get paid a salary of $70K to manage $1.5 million of revenue. If revenue drops below $1 million, maybe there is no bonus. You could also tier it down: at $1.25 million, *x* is the bonus; at $1 million, *y* is the bonus. In our example above of $1.5 million dropping to $750K, a business with a tiered bonus structure would survive. Why? The RM makes $70K (no bonus), the support person makes $70K, and an assistant makes $35K. That's $175K total, which, taken from $750K in revenue, yields $575K to the owner, less office rent and software expenses.

The second thing to do is identify secondary expenses, including nonessential personnel. Look at your P&L. Is there someone whose absence from your company would not affect the client's life? That's the real key. The last thing you want to show the client is that you're cutting people the client is relying on. Cutting secondary expenses means operations too. Look at your software and other technology expenses and decide what you could live without. Again, nothing you cut should affect a client's experience with your firm—*if possible*. Keep in mind that if you're not around, that affects the client even more.

The third way to prepare for a crash is to implement renegotiations with key vendors. One item to look at is your lease. This was a classic example in 2008 and 2009 of negotiations that could cut expenses. If the lease on your office space has eighteen months left, that doesn't help you right now because you need to cut expenses today. Go to the owner of your space and say, "I'll renew right now for another five years, but you've got to lower my cost to this." Remember, to a landlord that's going to be an attractive offer—he's facing a lot of empty office space because everyone is expecting real estate prices to crash like in 2008. In addition to your landlord, go through each of your key vendors and try to negotiate a deal down.

The fourth step to prepare for 2008 is to establish a line of credit you can draw on in times of extreme peril. If you need capital to keep key employees, for example, you could draw on that credit to get that capital. Markets do come back.

The fifth step is to build a business that is less correlated to drops like this. If your investments have downside protections, so does your business. You can even go as far as using corporate capital to maintain some shorts or out-of-the-money puts on the market to make sure you have the money to survive these downturns. Other industries like steel and agriculture do this all the time, so it's not so far-fetched.

The message here is to have a plan for a market crash. We are utterly shocked to see how many firms lack a plan that's written out and ready to go. We'd estimate that only one out of every hundred firms actually has a plan. And yet we know—we don't think, we know—that once every fifteen or twenty years a crash happens. Write a plan and be ready to implement it.

Your Philosophy on Paying Your People

We talked about the Moss Adams Advisor Compensation and Staffing Study,[21] which shows by job function what people are paid. Use this resource as a guideline for paying your team fair salaries. Have the study at hand to show employees so you can say, "This is what others in your position are earning." You can show them exactly where they stand in that pay range. If you don't want to use that study, custodians like Fidelity and Schwab have similar studies. IMCA also has a compensation study that is especially good.

Beyond paying your team fairly, you must have a philosophy around compensation. Just as you need to have a philosophy for financial planning and one for investment management, you need one for what you're going to pay people. Then you must commit to that philosophy. If people want to make more than that, maybe it's time for them to move on.

Beyond paying your team fairly, you must have a philosophy around compensation. Just as you need to have a philosophy for financial planning and one for investment management, you need one for what you're going to pay people.

Our philosophy was that people who had tenure with us deserved to be paid in the upper quartile of like positions in similar parts of the country. Location can't be overlooked because an operations manager in New York City earns twice as much as an operations manager in Cheyenne, Wyoming. We'd ask, "Does this person have some tenure with us? And are they past the point where we're training them and they're now starting to train us?"

21 "Moss Adams Advisor Compensation and Staffing Study," *Investment News*.

That was our philosophy on when people deserved to be in the upper quartile: they had been with us for a while, and we were no longer having to come up with all the answers for them. They had started to come up with answers on their own and were adding value to our firm.

For those folks, we'd open the Moss Adams study and say, "We think you're really good at what you do, and you deserve to be paid in the upper quartile of this position." We'd pick the middle of the upper quartile. If we didn't think they had gotten to the point where they were adding value, then we'd use the study and pay them in the second quartile and tell them what they needed to do to get to the upper quartile.

Our philosophy was clear, and we committed to it. It became very effective because it was clear and understandable. If someone came in and said, "My girlfriend makes blank at blank," we'd reply, "Well, here's the study. Here's the data." It put an end to the argument of whether or not people were being paid fairly.

There are a few other lessons we learned about paying people. Start lower to go higher. When we find someone we really like, we all have a tendency to offer them more so they will take the job. That's a shortcut. While it might get the job done faster, we're big fans of starting lower and training employees rather than trying to find people who demand a higher salary immediately.

Also, don't be afraid to walk away from an employee who is demanding more money. If you've gone through this process, you're paying that person in the upper quartile, and that person has been adding value but is not a revenue producer (not finding new business), at some point you will want to stand firm and see what that employee does. If you constantly give in to pressure, it's a no-win game. Everyone else on your team will see it. You've got to be willing to lose someone. Have a process and believe in it. If it costs you a person, so be it. Move on.

Don't Fall Victim to the "Grass is Greener" Mindset with Employees or Vendors

No one is happy with their employees all the time. Anyone who tells you they are is lying. But the mistake we see so many advisors make—and that we made early in our careers—is getting rid of a difficult employee because you think there's got to be somebody better out there. The cost of training a new employee, especially for operations staff, is enormous. *Financial Planning* writes, "Have you ever calculated the cost of hiring a new employee? It's not cheap. The average cost to a company of turning over a highly skilled job can be more than 200 percent of the annual compensation for that role once training costs, lost productivity, and hiring expenses are counted."[22]

When you turn somebody over, you've got to understand that the new person you're hiring reduces the efficiency of the rest of your team to that person's level. Getting the team up to speed and able to run at your pace takes a long time. Operations teams work in concert; a weak link affects everything. If you're opening new accounts, one person may be in charge of moving the money from the client's old advisor to your shop, another is in charge of loading all the data into the performance management system, and a third is in charge of creating new investments. So if the person processing all the paperwork isn't yet up to speed, everyone else experiences a slowdown while that person is being trained.

The lesson is to be careful about firing somebody on the assumption that the next person will necessarily be better. It's a chronic mistake we see made. Often it's better to retrain an employee rather than hire a new one. Be willing to invest in employee education.

22 Kelli Cruz, "Voices: Hiring Can Be a Bigger Cost Than Payroll if Not Done Right," *Financial Planning*, August, 27, 2018, https://www.financial-planning.com/opinion/how-financial-advisors-can-retain-employees.

Perhaps find a peer who has a person who is really good at the position for which your team member needs training. See if that peer will let your employee shadow that person for a week. There are other forms of employee education available at Barron's Team Summit and other annual conferences where people in each position share best practices.

The second place the grass is not always greener is vendors. We made the mistake of thinking that wire house B was better than wire house A, and if we just switched from A to B, everything would get better. Guess what? All the wire houses had the same problems. We also made the mistake of thinking that software vendor B was better than vendor A. In fact, A was better at some things, and B was better at others. By switching from A to B, all we did was create a new set of problems when we could simply have worked with vendor A to solve the old problems. We're not saying there's never a reason to make a change, just that you shouldn't believe that the grass is always greener. Most of the time it isn't.

The Importance of Family Meetings, Not Just Business Meetings

As you think about the balance of work and family, here is a test: are you nicer to someone in an outside business meeting than you are to your own family? When they do something that upsets you, do you react differently to the business acquaintance than you do to a member of your own family? We know we did. We were so tired by the time we got home, or so busy when a family member would call, or so used

As you think about the balance of work and family, here is a test: are you nicer to someone in an outside business meeting than you are to your own family?

to our staff doing tasks for us that we didn't treat them the same way we treated prospective clients. Somehow, our families forgave and loved blindly. Our failures were real, though, and we share this in the hope that you won't experience the same.

Everyone has "nice" in them. The question is where do you expend the limited amount of the resource we call "nice"? Do you use up your limited resource at work, or do you save some for the people who matter most? Consider how many hours you actually have for your family. There are 260 net working days in the year. Say you spend, on average, ten hours per day working and commuting. Hopefully you sleep eight hours, which leaves six hours for everything else. Those six hours represent 25 percent of your time. How can you save your resource of "nice" for that 25 percent? Not only is it the right thing to do for your family, but just see what happens in your business when your family is happy and functioning well versus when it's not. You'll see, like we did, that the 25 percent of your time you spend at home is the most important business time you have. All it takes is a little "nice."

The title of this chapter is "Running Your Practice Like a Business." You should make sure you're doing this planning process with your family as well. Most Type A personality advisors who have the ability to become high-performing advisors fail to recognize the impact their career has on their families.

Meg Hirshberg's *For Better or For Work: A Survival Guide for Entrepreneurs and Their Families* is likely the most painful book that any Type A business executive will ever read. But it's filled with crazy amounts of reality. Hirshberg's message, which changed our lives completely, is this: "Think about how many business meetings you have to work on your business, plan your business, and think about your business. Maybe you have twelve of these a year. Then ask yourself one simple question: when is the last time you had one of those meetings about your family?" Why shouldn't your family have goals, strategy meetings, and follow-ups? Why shouldn't you think about how you can help a family member grow the same way you think about a staff member or a client?

Our failure to do that early in our career cost us dearly in our relationships with family members. We made a midlife correction to get back on track, but we wish somebody had put Meg Hirshberg's book in front of us a long time ago. It's scarily true. She talks about meeting with your family regarding planning, values, and setting goals. Those are all words we use about our business. When *is* the last time you did that with your family? It's powerful stuff. Don't be a victim to our industry and the ridiculous divorce rate!

CHAPTER 8
HOW TO GROW YOUR PRACTICE

It's difficult to grow your practice if you aren't unique. Growth depends on finding your niche; everything else in this chapter is dependent on that. Once you've found your niche, you must be able to describe it in short order. Whether you call it an elevator pitch or a one-minute drill or something else, you must be able to distinctly tell someone how you're different than everyone else.

When we travel around the country talking to advisors, most tell us they have a niche, but when we ask them to describe it, we hear stumbling as they try to differentiate themselves. This is common whether or not the advisor is young or has been around a long time. In this business, because we are so busy, we spend very little time looking at exactly what it is that makes us unique, which is a mistake.

In the last chapter, we talked about how to run your practice like a business. The first step is creating a vision statement, which talks about what makes you unique. It answers the question, "What is your value proposition to clients?" When you know your niche and the value you're offering, you can be a true specialist serving the exact needs your prospective clients have. And, perhaps most important, you have pricing power.

At our firm, we helped clients who wanted to monetize their business and set up a family office. We built a detailed marketing plan around our niche, committed to it, and revisited it weekly. Our plan conveyed the message that we were unique because we had monetized businesses ourselves. We started six companies and sold all of them—taking one public and selling others to synergistic buyers and financial buyers—and we had set up our own family office and dealt with all the complications and problems of doing that, including responsibly transferring wealth to the next generation. Our vision statement fit into a fifteen-second elevator pitch: we help other people do what we did and learn from our mistakes. It was a clear message. We've been where you are, and that's why you want to hire us.

Some people get lost in the idea of a value statement. They overthink it, assuming it's asking for your deepest beliefs about the world. In this case, it's simply your value to the client. Understand that value, put together a clear and concise value statement, and then create a detailed marketing plan around it.

A Written Marketing Plan

You may think using the word *written* in the heading above is redundant—of course the marketing plan would be written, right? Yet, to our shock, most of the advisors who are facing this wall *know* what kind of clients they want, but when we ask them for the exact steps they're going to take to go after those clients, or why those clients will accomplish the firm's goals, *there is no written plan*. This is true of younger advisors, midcareer advisors, and older advisors.

To get new clients, Schwab's study underscores the importance of a written marketing plan: 75 percent of firms that have over $500 million AUM have a formal strategy to acquire new clients. If you want to get to that level or higher, you must have a marketing plan that says, "Here are the clients we're going after, and here is exactly how we're going to go after them. And once we find them, here is our value proposition that will cause them to understand why they should hire us."

Imagine you are some other business, like a consumer product company instead of a financial advisory firm. Say you sell furniture. You're going to sell to people who have houses, so you know who your customers are, but you have no idea how you're going to put your brand in front of those customers. How are you going to show that your product is different from everybody else's?

"I'll just sell furniture to people who have houses" is the marketing plan most advisors have. That's what we see looking at most independent firms. They say something like, "We're after ultrahigh net worth clients, and we're going to ask all our clients for referrals, and we're going to do a seminar every once in a while, and we're going to do client appreciation every once in a while."

That's not a marketing plan. A marketing plan details how many contacts you're going to create in specific time periods, how many referrals you're going to ask for, how many invites to seminars you're going to send out, what you expect your response rate to be, what you're going to say in the seminar, the number of people you expect to ask for appointments after the seminar, what you expect in conversion from prospects to clients and why they will choose you (value proposition), etcetera, etcetera, etcetera. A written marketing plan is detailed and comprehensive.

Fidelity's study on marketing showed that high-performing teams all have defined marketing plans: "Marketing leaders outpace other RIAs by a wide margin when it comes to creating, executing, and monitoring a plan."[23]

It's basic stuff, but in our industry, written marketing plans seem to be the exception, *not* the rule. You see fly-by-the-seat-of-your-pants

23 "Establishing a Growth Engine through Marketing and Business Development," *Fidelity*, 2014, https://clearingcustody.fidelity.com/app/proxy/content?literatureURL=/9863706.PDF.

plans. Why is this? It comes back to scaling and having the right team structure. In most independent firms, financial advisors are wearing so many darn hats. We're chief executive officer and chief investment officer and maybe even chief technical officer and chief marketing officer as well. No wonder marketing doesn't happen the way it should. When we're chief everything, we haven't developed a team structure where someone has specific responsibilities for marketing. We have not created the time in our day to envision a detailed plan, let alone the time to track it and improve it.

Most advisors we talk to know these steps we're talking about; they have read the books about how to write a plan. They know that they should have a written marketing plan. They know they need to track it and comp around it, but it doesn't get done. It's just that they don't have the time. Why don't they? They lack the right team structure.

You must identify someone within your team (other than yourself) who is responsible for building a marketing plan and executing it. The plan must lay out exactly how advisors will contact new clients (e.g., seminars, referrals, COIs) and what actions they will take every week to accomplish success (e.g., ask for five referrals per week and expect one prospective client meeting per week). This person does not have to build the plan without your input nor execute it without your help. After all, you're the rainmaker, but without dedicated time and personnel, this won't go well. The plan must be measured every week, and each member of the team must be accountable for four components:

1. Number of new clients closed
2. Number of new client appointments
3. Number of referrals requested
4. Number of "wow" actions completed to earn the right to ask for a referral

Marketing as a Culture

Once you have a marketing plan, you must follow it, measure it, and comp it. Shockingly, most firms that create marketing plans revisit those plans once a year. And they're surprised when that doesn't work. Following it means that at least once a month you revisit where you are by measuring what's working and what isn't. At our firm, we did that every single week.

Every action was measured. If we were doing an event, for example, we tracked the number of invites that went out and responses received, as well as where we were relative to budget expectations and what each team member needed to do in the next week. Detail and tracking are the key to success.

We had erasable walls in our office that had a special kind of paint you could write on and wash off easily. A whiteboard and dry-erase markers would work just as well. On one wall we listed every targeted name. We had an A list of prospective clients and a B list. The A list were those we had already been in contact with, made presentations to, and expected that we could get the deal done imminently. The B list were still prospects. We had that board in front of the entire team. We obviously kept it separate from the client area, but you couldn't walk in or out of where our team worked without seeing that board. Every time you got up to get coffee, you would see that board. It focused everyone around our values, our marketing plan, and what we needed to do to reach our goals.

Then we met weekly. In those marketing meetings, we asked where we were on each prospect and what we could do to move things forward. We also went through the B list and asked what we needed to do to move them up to A. Writing on the walls and meeting weekly about marketing may sound extreme, but the takeaway is that marketing is a culture. If you create a culture in your firm around this, you will be great marketers. As an owner in this business, you have to be driving marketing and making it a part of everybody's daily life. You have to get your team ingrained in that culture.

When you get a true culture, you can open up your thinking and accomplish even greater things. One of the finest people I ever got to work with—Michael Dieschbourg, now Head of Stewardship and Responsibility at Herme's—told us to "Just say yes!" This revolutionized how we thought. He was really saying listen to your customers, find their needs, and then go solve that need, and you will do more business. This is what lead us to the revolution that relationship alpha was the key to getting and keeping clients. It was what made us different and unique but, more importantly, kept our clients. When our culture was right, we were open to new ideas, and this caused us to change how we marketed ourselves, becoming "niche players."

There's more on how to pay for marketing later in the chapter, but your bonus structure should apply to your entire team, from relationship managers to operations staff. Comping means aligning people's compensation with marketing, and you do that up and down the organization. Everyone is on fixed salaries with a bonus structure. Whatever bonus they receive is tied to how the entire organization does in terms of retaining clients and getting new clients.

You might ask what a relationship manager or operations assistant has to do with marketing. Why would they be comped on that? Well, one of the best marketing resources is referrals. Who is in the best position to get referrals? It's those relationship managers. Keeping existing clients happy is, of course, the best way to get referrals. Who is in a great position to keep existing clients happy? It's operations people. You convince the team that as the team goes, everybody goes. It's not just how any one person performs; it's how the whole team performs.

One of our consulting clients once said to us, "All this sales stuff you push is just not us. We're not that kind of advisor." The next thing we said to him left him breathless: "Then you're a dinosaur, and you and the people around you are on your way to extinction."

We know … it sounds harsh! But this firm needed a reality adjustment. In this business, unlike other businesses, we don't have perpetual customers. Firms that don't have a marketing culture will tread water at best and eventually will fall by the wayside. The average life of a client relationship is seven to eight years. Regardless of how good an advisor you are, clients leave. Our business just has too much attrition over time to accomplish the goals in this book without having the marketing culture described above. One of the best firms we ever worked with said it this way: "Eat or be eaten."

Creating Presence

Any successful marketing plan has to have presence behind it. Just as it's difficult to grow your firm if you aren't unique, it's difficult to be a successful marketer without presence. A critical step to growing your practice is to create presence for yourself.

A critical step to growing your practice is to create presence for yourself.

Presence and niche sound similar, but you need to have one to have the other. To be niche means you specialize in something; to have presence means you are *known* for specializing in it. In short, you must be a recognized subject matter expert to have presence.

We have thirty-three years in this business. We are acknowledged widely in different publications and on television and radio. If we're going up against a thirty-two-year-old guy who doesn't have any of that publicity, what are the odds of that guy beating us? They're low. Not impossible, but low. Most clients are going to hire the advisor with all the presence around him. Charles Schwab surveyed 1,000 consumers and found that 97 percent of those with more than $250K in assets said a high level of expertise matters when selecting a financial advisor. *Financial Planning* writes, "So go ahead and tout years of experience in the field, your awards and achievements and any special certifications. That kind of salesmanship won't necessarily turn your clients off or come across as self-aggrandizing; instead it serves to build trust."[24]

To be niche means you specialize in something; to have presence means you are known for specializing in it.

Everybody says, "Well, good for you. You've got all this stuff that I don't. Thanks for shoving it in my face." What a lot of people don't realize is that you can *get* presence. They think you have to be lucky to get your name in magazines and newspapers, but that's not true at all. You can hire a PR firm to get placements. You can also buy media. There are numerous media outlets in our industry—including prestigious publications like *Forbes* and *Wealth* magazines—where you can buy space, and they make it look like an article that you published.

A lot of people think that they can't become a media personality, yet many high-performing advisors have used television and radio to market themselves as experts. All those people bought space; they didn't get there by chance. Another way to create presence for yourself is to become a teacher. Every college today is looking for adult education because it's an important revenue source for universities. Create a curriculum, go visit your local college or university, and tell them you want to teach a course. Some will actually market

24 Kerri Anne Renzulli, "Clients Care About Your Credentials More Than You Think," *Financial Planning*, October 2, 2018, https://www.financial-planning.com/news/charles-schwab-survey-clients-say-credentials-matter-when-picking-financial-advisors.

the course for you. But even if you had to market it yourself, now you're a college professor. That's presence.

Writing a book is a great way to create presence. Many advisors think writing a book takes too much time or they don't know how. But you don't have to know how. Ghostwriting companies can help you do this with a minimal investment of your time. Your ideas get turned into a published document that gives you authority and presence.

Marketing for Social Media and the Next Generation

Another way to market in our industry is to do what all the coaches are talking about: become an expert to millennials, who many think need to be talked to or treated in a different way. If you can be successful with those clients, it's certainly one way to grow your practice. Underlying the whole idea around millennials, however, is a more important point, which is whether or not social media can play a role in your marketing.

As time goes on, more and more financial advisors will be found through SEO methodologies. We believe that correctly positioning yourself online is extremely important. This is another aspect of presence. The key to SEO is getting mentioned in other people's articles so your name appears under a lot of searches. You drill down and use keywords such as "wealth management" or "how to manage money in retirement." Whatever your niche is.

So do we think people should do SEO research? Absolutely. It's an important step in any marketing plan. However, too many times we find that people think they should do this in order to market to millennials. We think people should do this whether they're marketing to millennials or not.

Even if you don't believe that clients search the web in order to find a financial advisor, we guarantee that clients search the web for reinforcement, both positive and negative, about *hiring* a financial advisor. People will Google your name and look to see who else thinks you're good. If magazines have written about you, this will serve you well. Of course, what we're describing with SEO is not earth-shattering. Everyone knows this stuff is important, so why aren't more teams doing it? It all comes back to time. If you don't have the right team structure around you, and you're having to be chief everything, there isn't time to market, or do SEO, or do many of the other things necessary to build a high-performing firm.

How to Pay for Marketing: Variable Versus Fixed Costs

Because our industry was brought up in a commission-based world, that mindset extends to marketing as well. We tend to want to pay marketing people with variable dollars. In other words, come work for us, and if you raise a whole bunch of money, then you'll get 20 percent of it, or maybe 30 or 40 percent.

Here's what you will find if you use that pay structure: the bad ones will still be bad, and the good ones will end up becoming real problems because you pay them so much money while they're not doing anything else on the team.

For example, say you're running a firm that has 50 percent profitability before you pay yourself as owner. For every $1 million brought in, you spend $500K to run the firm and $500K is profit. If you offer a marketing person 30 percent of that $1 million in revenue that he or she brings in—i.e., $300K—you now have only $700K, which leaves you with $200K in profit. Your marketing person is making more than you are on the next $1 million. Of course, as companies grow there are economies of scale, but the point is still true.

We regularly use this kind of example with clients, and they marvel at it when they think about paying people with a variable pay structure. Yet people in the industry still do it because nobody wants to spend money for a lack of success. They do it because they're trying to avoid having money flowing out the door with no results to show for it. But if you're going to grow your business, you're going to have to take some risks.

You might ask how we can be so sure of this. The scenario above, in which your marketing person ends up making more than you, happened to us. We hired a marketing guy on variable pay. He was successful, but he managed no client relationships. We tried to have him manage relationships, but that just wasn't his skill set. Clients complained because they weren't getting the right kind of service. We had a large amount of money going out the door every month whether our marketing guy came to work or not. He wasn't servicing accounts, yet he was still getting paid. It makes it very hard to reward the people doing the work when 20–30 percent of revenue goes out the door to people who aren't helping run the business every day.

Having our marketing person on variable pay became unprofitable. This was a real "aha" moment for us. If you pay people on a variable scale—still the standard in the industry—it may not turn out the way you think. In fact, great success can be the worst thing that happens to you. We know because we lived it.

So how do you include everyone? Create a bonus pool. When we were starting this process, it was 5 percent of gross revenue and over time became 10 percent of EBOC. So a $2 million advisor doing 50 percent EBOC or net income before he/she pays themselves would put $100K into the pool.

Step 2 is use your Marketing Plan. It has a stated goal of NNA (Net New Assets). Ours was always $70 million for the last fifteen years or so. It was aggressive on purpose and because we knew it could be done if we had the right culture of marketing. Whatever number you use, the full $100K becomes available when that is reached. Each person's eligible component was their percent of the company total compensation without owner's compensation. So if your RM is 40 percent of the total compensation, he or she would get $40K.

Another model has salary being up or down by the growth or fall in the firms EBOC. In this model people get a base salary that can never be violated, but if net income doubles, so does salary. Before you say it won't work, do the math because it will work and create the culture you want.

Don't Make Pricing a Marketing Strategy

We fell victim to the idea that clients are extremely price conscious. The thinking goes that if you just price correctly, you will end up getting more clients. Well, maybe we did win a few extra clients because we were pricing low, but at the end of the day, profitability will come back to haunt you. Fidelity notes in its RIA Benchmarking Study that widespread discounting is driving down revenue.[25]

Once we had presence in the industry—once we were recognized as experts in our niche—price was no longer an issue. We would win business because we were the most qualified to handle that business. This was another "aha" moment for us: it can become a big mistake to let price become a sales strategy. If you don't get it right to begin with, you'll end up paying for a long time into the future. Some of our biggest clients who took the most time were acquired on discounted fee schedules. A $20 million account paying twenty basis points still yields $40K in revenue, just like a $4 million account paying 1 percent.

25 "Growth, Productivity, and Profitability: Maximize Your RIA Firm's Harvest," *Fidelity Investments*, 2017, https://clearingcustody.fidelity.com/app/proxy/content?literatureURL=/9882273.PDF.

But the $20 million account needs and wants a lot more attention and services. In short, discounting hurts your ability to scale.

Scale Operations to Marketing Success

Think of being in the role of operations manager. You're getting paid $80K, $90K, or $100K a year to be the backbone of the team. As the firm's marketing efforts bring in more clients, you're setting up the paperwork systems for all of them. You see your workload increasing. For everyone else in the organization, if their pay is tied to marketing, they will make more money. But if the operation manager's pay is not tied to marketing, then they're working harder for the same salary.

Everybody has to participate in marketing, and everybody has to get paid for participating. Marketing becomes a culture that permeates your organization.

No employee is going to be happy with that scenario. You need to pay your entire team the same way. Everybody has to participate in marketing, and everybody has to get paid for participating. Marketing becomes a culture that permeates your organization.

***

All the marketing strategies we talked about in this chapter will grow your business organically. But they pale in comparison to what we'll cover in the next chapter: inorganic growth—i.e., the marketing opportunity created through mergers and acquisitions.

CHAPTER 9
HOW TO GROW THROUGH M&A

Bigger independent firms rely less on marketing and more on referral and M&A to grow. Why? Because they have become specialists in their niche and have the right model to scale. According to Cerulli Associates' RIA report, teams doing $2 million in revenue focus *more* on marketing than teams doing $5 million.[26] The bigger teams are able to gather more assets by referral and M&A.

For most firms, organic growth cannot hold a candle to the power of M&A. Consider acquiring a firm that has 150 households. That would be an average firm doing $2 million in revenue, and there's a boatload of those firms out there. If you can buy a firm with 150 households, the question any advisor should ask is: how many meetings with prospects would you need in order to generate 150 new clients?

Think about how much time it takes with a prospect before they actually become a client. You need to factor in how many hours it takes you to generate a lead, how many hours it takes you in the sales process to close an account, and what your close ratio is from prospect to client.

Let's say it takes four hours of your firm's time to generate a lead. Sometimes that time is getting everything ready to ask for a referral;

26 Cerulli Associates, "The Cerulli Report: U.S. RIA Marketplace 2017: Ascendance of the Billion-Dollar Firm," 2017, accessed August 2019.

sometimes it's playing golf or going to a cocktail party. Regardless, if you close 50 percent of the prospects who agree to meet with you, that means it takes eight hours of your time to land one new prospect. Therefore, in total hours, if you're going to get 150 new clients, that's 150 clients multiplied by eight hours per client, or 1,200 hours. Put another way, 1,200 hours, working eight hours per day, is 150 days of work.

To generate 150 new clients you would need 150 days when you're doing nothing but marketing. The average firm in our industry spends around 10 percent of their time on marketing. There are about 230 working days in the year. Ten percent of 230 is twenty-three days. With that amount of time dedicated to marketing each year, it would take six and a half years to put in 150 days of marketing and generate 150 new clients—and this all assumes you can find 150 new prospects and doesn't count the time it took you to plan and follow up on marketing campaigns.

The same thing can be accomplished in one M&A transaction. Most nonhigh-performing teams without a detailed marketing plan add around ten new households a year. Go back over the last three years at your firm and be honest about how many new households you added each year. Even if you're adding fifteen new households each year, it would take ten years of prospecting to get 150 new clients. Organic growth simply cannot hold a candle to M&A.

Four Keys to M&A Success

Now that we can see the benefit of M&A from a marketing and growth perspective, let's take a look at what is needed to be successful.

First, it requires resources. Resources are divided into two groups: money and people. The money part is obvious. If you're going to go buy a firm, you need the capital to do it. We'll talk later in the chapter about where that capital comes from.

The less obvious part is people, which most firms overlook. Not having someone on the team dedicated to M&A is a mistake. M&A is a full-time job. At our prior firm, we had one full-time employee whose entire job was marketing and M&A. It takes that much time to work on deals and see them through. With that said, we do think that one marketing person can lead both organic (the strategies we discussed in our last chapter) and M&A marketing with advisor support.

Second, you must have a team structure that can absorb the clients acquired through an M&A deal. You need enough bench strength among your relationship managers, who must be experienced advisors capable of taking on these new accounts. In other words, they need excess capacity. If your RMs are already handling $1.5–2 million of revenue, then you need to acquire existing advisors in the buyout. M&A is a great way to acquire new talent. Brent Brodeski, the CEO of Savant Capital Management, one of the nation's leading RIAs, put it this way: "The reality is the best people are hard to get; they're not standing on a street corner waving a résumé and saying, 'Hire me.' So if you can't hire them, you can add them by merging with another firm."[27] Failing to have bench strength will limit your success because sellers will eventually ask how you can handle their clients when you're already fully booked.

Third, you must have an operational system that is set up and streamlined for growth. It is critical to have a successful operational platform to have a successful M&A strategy with one of the keys being built-in workflows to handle the account opening process.[28] Put another way, you need the technology behind you to add 150 new households, plug them into a system that works, and keep track of them.

Ninety-eight percent of advisors say having an "efficient and

---

27 Paikert, "Why Building a Multibillion Dollar Firm is Not for the Faint of Heart."

28 "M&A Through the Operational Lens," *Wealth Management*, June 28, 2018, https://www.wealthmanagement.com/white-papers/ma-through-operational-lens.

scalable back office is very or extremely important when integrating firms."[29] At the heart of this system is an operational platform that creates accountability and streamlines work. Firms that are successful in M&A have the people in place, but they also have the systems that tell them what to do each day. You must have a contact resource management system, or CRM, that keeps track of this massive influx of new relationships and tells your team what needs to be done and when. If you're used to absorbing ten new accounts a year and suddenly you bring on 150 all at once, can you imagine how your system could get overloaded?

Firms that are successful in M&A have the people in place, but they also have the systems that tell them what to do each day.

Your CRM must be able to handle and track the onboarding of new relationships. The idea is to build out workflows that function through your CRM. A high-functioning CRM has finalized workflows for the account opening process. When a prospect becomes a client, the CRM assigns a new account to the team. It tells operations to generate new account paperwork. Next, it tells the advisor that the paperwork has been completed, so it's their responsibility to meet with the client and get it signed. Or it might tell an assistant to schedule the prospect to come in and sign. Once the paperwork is signed, operations processes it, and the system auto-creates a welcome letter followed by, one week later, a "touch piece" that says, "I'm reviewing your accounts and thought you would find this interesting." Additionally, the system schedules the first meeting and follow-up meetings and reminds the

29 "[Infographic] Surfing the Wealth Management M&A Wave," *Wealth Management*, June 28, 2018, https://www.wealthmanagement.com/technology/infographic-surfing-wealth-management-ma-wave.

RM to update the client's financial plan. To onboard successfully, it's all driven primarily through your CRM.

The good news is that the systems exist, and they can be bought or outsourced as discussed earlier. You just need to make that a priority—60 percent of advisors say bulk transfer of new clients is a challenge second only to cultural alignment.[30] Prioritizing systems and bulk onboarding is a step many firms skip and therefore struggle with later in the M&A process. This can come back to haunt you, especially with systems, because of the sheer amount of onboarding you have to do.

Lastly, you need an investment team in place because you are taking on someone else's investment management responsibilities. When you're doing M&A work, the whole idea is to take the firm that you are acquiring and roll them into the way you manage money and handle clients. But it doesn't happen that way immediately. On day one, you have firm A and firm B; firm A invests one way, and firm B invests another way. You need an investment team to migrate that process from one firm to the other.

Technology and Vendors for Bulk Onboarding

So we know one of the key successes to M&A is having a robust operational platform because with any M&A deal, you're going to be opening hundreds of new accounts. A key question to ask would be this: what other things can assist me other than my platform? With a robust process, you can push the workload out to vendors. You're looking to utilize vendors' ability to bulk upload as much as possible. If you have 150 new households, you're not going to want to physically upload each one of those contacts into your CRM system. You manage the data dealing with those 150 households—a spreadsheet with contact information, prior notes, etc., that you received from

30 "[Infographic] Surfing the Wealth Management M&A Wave," *Wealth Management*.

the selling firm—but then you hand that data off to your CRM vendor to generate those new clients in your CRM database.

Do the same thing with your reporting platform. With 150 new households, you need to track each account, create new reports, and assign billing definitions. But to get these resources, you must develop strong relationships with your vendors so they will allocate resources when you need them.

Morningstar Office, Orion, Tamarac, Envestnet, Junxure and Redtail are just some of the big players in this vendor area. You hire one of these companies and utilize some or all of their platform offerings. They take on the bulk updates for you.

Synergy Cost Elimination

We reviewed what it takes to be successful at M&A, but we haven't looked at the impact of an M&A deal from a financial perspective. As you can see in the chart, we use an example of a buying firm that currently has $5 million in revenue, a 60 percent profit margin including owner's salaries, and a 75 percent profit margin when looking at earnings before owner's compensation (EBOC), which is right in line with industry standards for high-performing firms. This buyer is looking to purchase a firm that is currently producing $1.2 million in revenue and has a profit margin of 35 percent including owner's salaries and a 56 percent profit margin when calculating EBOC.

When buying a firm, we typically purchase based on the firm's current net income before the owner takes any compensation. In other words, we base our multiple on the current EBOC of the firm—in this case, 56 percent or $675K. The beauty of this is once we acquire the firm (assuming we are acquiring and merging them into our current platform and cost centers), we are able to eliminate additional costs (synergies) in the selling firm, such as rent, staff

SYNERGY COSTS AND THE BENEFITS OF M&A					
	Buying Firm Current PL	Firm being Acquired PL (Pre-sale)	Firm Being Acquired PL (EBOC Calculation & Valuation Price)	Firm Being Acquired PL (Post Sale/ Eliminating Synergy Costs)	Buying Firm PL Post Purchase
Gross Revenue	$5,000,000	$1,200,000	$1,200,000	$1,200,000	$6,200,000
Owners Salary	$750,000	$250,000	-	-	$750,000
Admin and Payroll	$500,000	$250,000	$250,000	$125,000	$625,000
Healthcare	$75,000	$50,000	$50,000	$25,000	$100,000
Rent	$100,000	$75,000	$75,000	-	$100,000
Reporting Costs	$75,000	$25,000	$25,000	$20,000	$95,000
Compliance Legal	$75,000	$50,000	$50,000	$10,000	$85,000
Accounting	$20,000	$15,000	$15,000	$15,000	$35,000
Other Admin Expenses	$430,000	$60,000	$60,000	$25,000	$455,000
Total Expenses	$2,025,000	$775,000	$525,000	$220,000	$2,245,000
Net Profitability	$2,975,000	$425,000	$675,000	$980,000	$3,955,000
Profit Margins	60%	35%	56%	82%	64%

costs, benefits, administration, and office expenses, some legal and accounting, and some reporting. After we acquire the firm and eliminate these synergy costs (costs we are already paying today for our own firm with the right team structure), we are able to increase profitability to 82 percent, or $980K, of revenue.

It is important to note that this is an example, but it shows the power of M&A. We were able to purchase a firm for $635K and now operate it at $980K, giving us an additional $345K of operating cash flow to help pay for the transaction or hit the bottom line. After the purchase has occurred and been paid for by eliminating these expenses, we are able to increase margins in the firm by nearly 5 percent in a single transaction and increase our profitability from $2.725 million to $3.705 million (assuming all things are constant).

Where Does the Money Come From?

Most deals are done with seller financing. You can generally buy firms in our industry with 20 percent down. Let's use the example of a firm doing $2 million in revenue. If 50 percent of that $2 million falls to the bottom line, they're doing $1 million EBOC (earnings before owner's compensation). Typically, a firm with $1 million EBOC would be sold for three times that value, or $3 million. That's the purchase price. Of that $3 million, you have to pay 20 percent down, so you're spending $600K up front. The remaining $2.4 million will be paid to the selling firm over four or five years, which works out to $480K–600K a year. This is called seller financing because the seller is financing the purchase. Many deals, but not all, are done with this structure. This is the best deal for the buyer in that the business may pay for the remaining purchase after year one.

If the seller won't finance or you need the capital for the initial payment, you can find a bank loan. There are banks that specialize in this kind of lending. The rates are competitive; you should be able to borrow at the prime lending rate, or prime plus one, if you're a solid firm. Live Oak is one example of a bank designed to serve this marketplace. These banks truly understand financial advisors and the M&A model.

However, using a bank loan to finance a deal comes with a big caveat: 100 percent of these transactions (that we have seen) require personal guarantees from the owners of the companies, as well as a substantial net worth that is generally two or three times what you are borrowing. In the $3 million example above, if the seller won't do seller financing and you decide to pay them up front, you still put down that 20 percent, or $600K, and then borrow the additional $2.4 million. To borrow $2.4 million, you would need a net worth of two to three times that amount, or between $4.8 million and $7.2 million. Very few deals are 100 percent up front, but the point is what it takes to get financing. Keep in mind that financing can take two to four months to get done your first time, which means preparing well in advance.

The third and final way to raise the capital to acquire another firm is to bring in a partner who has capital. This is generally done using an aggregator like Focus Financial, PCG, or Dynasty. A company like this will bring capital to the table for a piece of your firm. In short, you're selling part of your firm to the aggregator, and they provide the capital so you can go buy other firms. Some firms like Dynasty are running innovative hybrid models where they will loan money if they are engaged with you for back-office services.

Like the banks, these firms charge interest on the money used to buy other firms—but usually at better rates. Most will require a structure that pays back capital in five years. But the key is they own part of your firm now, so you have less cash flow to service the debt. What's more, most aggregators are not active in your business, which means you are paying out cash to a shareholder who doesn't take on any day-to-day workload. Further, many of these deals are structured on a preferred basis, meaning they get paid first dollars, which increases your risk in a downturn.

Presence, Success, and Similar Beliefs

You can have the people and systems and money, yet you will still fail at getting M&A deals done if you don't have presence. There has to be something special about you and your firm. The seller will eventually ask, "Why sell to you versus somebody else?"

There are lots of ways to get presence. You can be a writer, a speaker, or a teacher, but you must be a specialist who has presence. A M&A prospect is just like any other prospect. You have to convince them that you are the right fit for their clients. Ultimately, a selling advisor has to explain to their clients why he or she did this. Seventy-two percent of advisors say that "delivering a superior customer experience is a key reason to join forces with another firm."[31]

You can have the people and systems and money, yet you will still fail at getting M&A deals done if you don't have presence. There has to be something special about you and your firm. The seller will eventually ask, "Why sell to you versus somebody else?"

If you have not yet identified your niche and become a specialist in that space, you won't be successful in M&A. If two firms are competing for an acquisition, the advisor who is selling is going to choose the firm that he or she thinks will handle his or her clients best. That advisor doesn't always choose the higher price. The best fit is often much more important than price. If you demonstrate presence, that seller will believe in who you are and that you're the best fit for their clients.

31 "[Infographic] Surfing the Wealth Management M&A Wave," *Wealth Management*.

In addition to presence, you must be a firm that has had some success. It's difficult to acquire another firm if yours is struggling or still young. If a firm's assets under management are $50 million or $100 million, there haven't been a lot of things written about it; there aren't many accolades that demonstrate credibility. That firm will struggle to get a deal completed. You must have had some success to get sellers interested in selling to you. That way, they can tell their clients why they chose you.

In addition to presence and success, you need two firms with similar beliefs. For example, let's say the selling firm believes that the way to manage money is through a formal financial planning process. They never consider the use of commission-based products because they believe it to be a conflict of interest. The buyer's philosophy is different. They think annuities and life insurance have a place in financial planning; they don't believe it's a conflict of interest as long as it's fully disclosed, and, in fact, they think advisors who don't use all available solutions do a disservice to the client. The chances of these two firms seeing eye to eye are less than 50 percent and probably less than 25 percent. There's just too big of a river between what they believe about managing money.

Here's another example of differing beliefs. The selling firm believes that the way to create and manage money is to be fully invested in equities or stocks—i.e., to be a long-term investor with the mindset that markets always perform eventually. In contrast, the acquiring firm believes in using modern technology to decide when to be in the markets and when not to be; it uses research to find exotic investments that might still go up when markets go down. These two firms are not going to see eye to eye. There's going to be a river between them.

We've found ourselves on the other side of the river from a firm we thought matched. We pursued a firm we thought was the perfect fit for us. It was a bunch of CPAs who had gotten into managing money for clients. Their core business was accounting; their side business was wealth management. Our core business was wealth management; our side business was being tax efficient. Merging our practices seemed like a great marriage. We would take over wealth management and then refer all of our wealth management clients to their tax practice.

The problem was they saw asset management as an exercise in tax efficiency. Every decision they made about managing money was based on taxes. That's not how we operated. We managed money by creating a real return—i.e., dividends and interest. They thought that was paying taxes for no reason. We had a river between us. Another firm came along that was also made up of CPAs. We had been working on the deal for five years, and they got it done in two months. Why? Because they saw the world exactly the same way.

We spent a lot of time chasing someone who was never going to marry us. It's important to understand what it takes to be successful in M&As because too many firms spend too much time chasing deals that are never going to happen if core beliefs are fundamentally different. Don't chase firms that don't share your beliefs. They're always going to sell to someone more aligned with their philosophy.

M&A is about "economics and emotion," says Mark Cooper, CEO of Beacon Pointe Advisors. If deal structures are similar, "you have to give sellers a personal reason where they fit best."[32]

Small Versus Large M&A Transactions

This section should be an eye-opener for most readers because everything talked about in the industry is bigger and bigger deals. The aggregators, which are really venture capital shops, talk about how you've got to do bigger and bigger and bigger deals. We disagree.

32 Paikert, "Why Building a Multibillion Dollar Firm is Not for the Faint of Heart."

Smaller deals can be just as enticing. Before we explain why, first let's talk about why everyone pushes for bigger deals.

Focusing on bigger deals is common in the industry because of the work involved to do one transaction. It requires so much from your staff, especially relationship managers and the senior owner, that if you acquire a firm that has only $500K in revenue, the perception is you can't make it profitable. Common wisdom says if it takes the same amount of time to buy a firm that does $500K in revenue as a firm that does $10 million in revenue, why would you ever spend the time on the less lucrative firm?

This logic makes sense, but competition for that big firm could be a problem. The higher the revenue a firm has, the more buyers will be interested. A firm doing $4 million in revenue will have three to five times as many buyers interested as the firm doing $500K in revenue. There are *many* more people chasing the larger deals, and they often can pay more because their model is different arbitraging funds. They use the aggregator model discussed above.

Everybody thinks you've got to do bigger and bigger deals. But we argue that doing a few of these smaller deals can get you to the same place as long as you have the right infrastructure to support them. There's just much less competition going after the smaller firms. Further, many of the smaller firms are less profitable, which means you're buying at a better value and create the most synergy cost reductions.

It's *not* wasting your time to do a $500K deal and here's why: a firm doing $500K is much easier to absorb. A $500K firm would have around fifty relationships (if the average firm charges 1 percent in fees and the average account is $1 million, that's $10K per account; $500K in revenue divided by $10K per account is fifty accounts). It's far easier to bring on fifty relationships instead of 150.

You also pay a lot less for a smaller firm. A firm with $500K in gross revenue is probably making $200K. If you pay two times that, the value of the firm you're buying is $400K. If you're putting 20 percent down, that's only $80K. It's much more affordable to acquire smaller firms. And remember, you're still bringing on fifty new relationships. If your firm averages ten new relationships a year and you suddenly get fifty relationships, you just did five years of prospecting in one transaction.

Mergers: Challenges & Benefits

There's another reason the bigger firms focus on large transactions. We've been talking about acquiring, but there is enormous synergy in combining two large firms or one large firm with a slightly smaller firm. A lot of consolidator shops are merging firms doing $10 million and $5 million respectively.

But don't ignore smaller deals either—it's just that the smaller deals don't get the same PR. The whole idea of the consolidator is to get one of these $10 million firms and then merge in smaller firms. The reason you see so many big deals happening is because they need larger firms to represent the base of their platform so they can go acquire smaller firms around them. You don't hear about these smaller transactions, but they're happening every day. Don't be fooled by media reports that make it look like only big deals are being done. It's just the big deals get the PR.

Don't be fooled by media reports that make it look like only big deals are being done. It's just the big deals get the PR.

Merging is easier than acquiring because it doesn't require capital at the outset. Nor does it involve an enormous amount of risk because you're not putting capital out that you might lose. So why not just combine a bunch of firms and get those economies of scale? On the face of it, maybe you should, but make sure you don't fall victim to the mindset we've talked about in previous chapters, the idea that the grass is always greener. It's very easy to fall into that trap.

When you merge, you're merging personalities. All the good firms have their own personality, culture, and vision. When you bring that to bear with another firm, those personalities, cultures, and visions often conflict. Eight out of ten times, one firm's culture will survive and one won't.

There are exceptions, of course. There are people who know how to merge cultures and keep the best of each. But that takes two parties willing to find the middle ground that is better than either half. In an industry made up of Type A personalities, finding the middle ground is not easy.

In addition to the culture clash, another problem with mergers is getting fair valuations. To merge, you have to figure out what equity Company A will have and what Company B will have. If A and B are each doing $2 million a year of revenue, you might say each side gets 50 percent. Well, what happens if Company A is growing 25 percent a year and Company B is declining 10 percent a year—is that equity still 50/50? With mergers, determining a company's worth can be challenging.

Next comes the problem of buying out a minority partner. If the advisor you merged with wants to be bought out after five years, you still come to the point where you've got to put out capital. Maybe it's a lot less risk because two firms are together, but a merger still requires you to put out capital eventually.

At the same time, mergers have a big upside. You can eliminate an amazing amount of duplicative costs. Most of those savings come in real estate and people, but cost reductions of $250K for $1 million in gross revenue are often found, sometimes as much as $500K per $1 million. If yours is the surviving firm, merging is a safe way to acquire because by the time you have to buy out the minority partner, you've already got everything in the folds of your firm. There's not a lot of risk. Plus, of course, you didn't have to come up with the money at the beginning.

In addition to mergers, FP Transitions notes other, creative approaches to acquisitions outside of the "traditional transition of clients from one advisor to another." These include continuity partnerships, the sell and stay model, partial book acquisition, and joint venture/strategic alliance. "There's no denying that acquiring a book of clients is the fastest way to grow your business," writes FP's Rachel Beckwith. "Luckily, there are many strategies to achieving this goal, and there is likely one that will work for you, whatever your current situation is, if you know what opportunities to look for."[33]

If you are thinking of buying, merging or otherwise, we highly recommend you retain someone who has been there before, someone who can tell you about the upsides and pitfalls of each option from real-life experience like what we do at Lumina.

Finding Sellers

Once you have the people, process, presence, and money, the next step is to build a marketing plan around finding your ideal seller. We call this a seller profile.

Far too many firms go after sellers without really knowing what they're looking for. You'll want to consider firms that share your values, so there won't be a river between you. There is a ceiling on how large a firm you can afford to acquire. And you will probably

33 Rachel Beckwith, "Creative Acquisition Approaches," *FP Transitions*, August 8, 2018, https://www.fptransitions.com/blog/creative-acquisition-approaches.

want to find a firm that is at the right life cycle stage. You've got to figure out what this firm looks like.

At our firm, for example, we looked only for sellers who wanted an exit. The reason we focused on advisors who wanted to retire was because we didn't want any ongoing legacy issues. We weren't looking for new partners; we were just looking for new revenue. So we wanted to acquire an advisor who was going to the leave the business after a year or so. That way, we didn't have to merge their culture into our culture. We didn't have all the problems inherent in trying to bring on new staff.

It's crucial to figure out the seller profile, which should have three components. First, it must identify the size of the firm. This amount of revenue should not be more than 80 percent of your current revenue because you probably won't be successful above that. Meaning, if your firm is doing $1 million in revenue, you're not going to be successful buying a firm doing $3 million in revenue. Second, it must identify if you're trying to acquire talent. Do you want to buy a firm that has relationship managers who will come over in the buyout? Do you want to prize mergers over true acquisitions? Or do you already have enough bench strength in your firm? Third, it must identify your resource limitations. You need to have cash for at least 20 percent of the purchase in addition to excess capacity among your relationship managers and operations staff.

Once you've identified the ideal firm, the next step is figuring out how you're going to find sellers that fit this profile. The traditional method is hiring somebody like a business broker to locate these firms. That hasn't been enormously successful, but it is a way.

The best way to find sellers is to know what your niche is and then concentrate on other firms in the same niche. If you're a specialist in college endowments and foundations, then focus on firms that are also specialists in that area. If you're a certified financial planner, go to CFP meetings and look for firms that are CFPs. If your firm specializes in clients within a certain religious base, go to a trade show that focuses on that. We've found this method of finding sellers to be successful because you can be extremely focused, limiting the number of people you're trying to contact. When you start talking to a firm that shares your niche, you're instantly qualified because you're both in the same business.

A great way to find sellers is to utilize your peer group. Whether you're focused on mergers, acquiring talent, or retiring advisors, your peer group likely has all of these.

Another way to find sellers is through listing services. FP Transitions and Successions Link are examples of listing services for financial advisors who are selling. These services act like real estate brokers by identifying a firm for sale and sending that listing to thousands of financial advisors who may be interested in acquiring. You probably won't find a billion-dollar practice for sale on these listing services; you will find many firms that have $50 million or $200 million in assets under management.

The problem with the listing services is competition. You're competing against everyone under the sun—literally thousands, if not tens of thousands, of financial advisors who have seen that same listing. We have completed transactions using this method, but you must be ready to pay top price due to the competition and do it their way because these services are very "cut and paste" shops. They have a way of running transactions that works for them, so they like buyers who will work within their system.

Another way to find selling firms is to use vendors. Custodians are a great source for finding RIAs who have asked about options for exiting the business. Virtually every custodian has a department that works with RIAs looking for succession planning or monetizing.

The surprise is that few RIAs in acquisition mode use custodians and other vendors as a resource for finding firms that are trying to sell. Some of our best leads over the years were found by money managers—i.e., people we had hired to manage a client's money. They knew a lot about our firm, and they referred us to firms they knew were looking for a succession plan or monetization. It's the same idea with software providers and other vendors. You must be close to your vendors and develop those relationships in order to get referrals.

Another source is your employees. Most of your employees were not homegrown; they came from other financial advisors. Ask who they know from their past. A lot of them started in the wire house world, and eventually the advisor they worked for went out on their own. Offer them a small fee for calling their old advisor and saying, "I really like this firm, and they are out aggressively buying other advisors, so I thought of you."

The last way to find sellers is the wire houses themselves. You can acquire advisors who work inside a wire house. You hear about advisors going from one wire house to another, which is no different than a wire house advisor going to your firm. This kind of transaction has other kinds of risk than we've described in this chapter. You need some clearly specialized work to go after that kind of acquisition. But on the plus side, wire house advisors are usually larger and more experienced. If one of your goals is to build bench strength by bringing in advisors with talent, wire houses are a great place to look for advisors who are not producing enough revenue and will likely have their payout cut. They need to move, you build bench strength, and you will pay almost nothing for them.

Any of these ways to find sellers require you to get on the phone and start contacting people. Many firms dedicated to M&A have full-time calling staff, as mentioned earlier.

What Do You Pay for a Firm?

In an ideal M&A transaction, you want the seller to share the risk. We wouldn't do a transaction if that wasn't the case. In some transactions all cash is paid up front; in others some cash is paid up front, and the rest is paid on a guaranteed note on the back end over four or five years. We don't ever do either of those transactions no matter how good the book of business is. Guaranteed payments mean the seller has no skin in the game. It's a rule for us that the seller participates. He or she must have some of the risk in selling the business because he or she has the client relationships.

Guaranteed payments mean the seller has no skin in the game.

We prefer a transaction structure that has 20–40 percent paid up front, and the remaining 60–80 percent is paid based upon whether the seller's clients stay. If we're acquiring a $2 million firm with $1 million in profitability before owner's compensation, the firm would be valued at three times its profitability, or $3 million. Twenty percent up front is $600K. The remaining $2.4 million would be divided by four years to pay off the balance, so that's $600K a year for four years. But we would adjust that $600K up or down based on whether the clients stayed. If clients leave, revenue goes down, so we'll pay less. If the seller is able to increase those account sizes or refer us new business, then we would increase what we pay.

Let's say that $2 million firm we acquired lost value because half the clients left. If that firm is now doing only $1 million in revenue the second year after being acquired, instead of paying $600K that year, we'd pay half, or $300K. Likewise, if that $2 million firm refers new business that allows revenue to grow to $3 million, instead of paying $600K, we'd now pay $900K, or a 50 percent increase.

We want the selling advisor to participate on both the upside and downside. If a seller won't participate in that kind of transaction, you should be concerned. They must not be very confident in their business if they're not willing to share the risk.

Don't Lose the Golden Egg

We close this chapter with a warning. Everything about M&A sounds really exciting, but there are risks you can't control. The classic example is 2008. You could have done everything right acquiring a business in 2007 but then been destroyed in 2008 and 2009. You must model out a worst-case scenario—i.e., the market falls by 40–60 percent—to make sure your firm can live through it. Don't let any acquisition kill the whole operation. When we were doing a lot of M&A at our firm, we had a partner who would say to us, "Try not to lose the golden egg here." It's an important message. Make sure you model it out so even if this thing goes sour and you lose 50 percent of revenue, your business is still intact. The adjustable model discussed above helps that a great deal.

CHAPTER 10
THE CHOICES YOU MAKE

In our industry, advisors are called "talent." Talent can be bought and sold. Think of how the National Football League and Major League Baseball trade players. You may read about a football player whose contract is up; he's got a long history with the team, he holds a number of records, and the fans love him—but then he leaves to take more money to play with another franchise. The exact same thing happens in this industry. The wire houses are constantly out stealing players from other teams. At the same time, they regularly experience players defecting from their team for another.

Most anyone in the wire house world who is talented and does a lot of business will be highly sought after by other wire houses. When a team's starting quarterback leaves them, they just hire another quarterback from another team. It's talent, and they can always go hire more of it. In recent years, advisors who are at $1–2 million and hitting the proverbial wall can get paid double their revenue by switching teams. If they're producing $3–4 million in revenue, they may triple it. To put it back in sports' vernacular, it's a signing bonus.

You can imagine how attractive that is to many advisors. Take an advisor who's forty years old and doing $2 million in revenue. Somebody's going to write him a check for $4–6 million? He's got a mortgage on his house and college educations to pay for. You can see how enticing it would be to jump ship and take that offer.

As a result, a tremendous number of advisors switch teams in the wire house world. In an effort to curb this, the wire house industry recently started dismantling something called "protocol," a legalized system to allow this kind of poaching. Again, it's very similar to the NFL and MLB: there are rules about when you can steal a player from another team, and if you do it the wrong way, there are repercussions, like having to give up draft choices. In our industry, if you followed protocol, there were no repercussions for stealing talent from another firm. But if you didn't follow protocol, then one party might sue the other.

For decades now, the wire houses have all stolen talent from one another. Now that the industry is starting to change this, it's harder and less lucrative for these advisors to move from one wire house to another. This is going to increase the trend of advisors leaving wire houses and setting up their own shops. A recent white paper from BNY Mellon confirms this: "Today nearly twice as many advisors serve their clients from an independent RIA than just ten years ago."[34] This trend is also an opportunity for independents to jump in and acquire talent as wire houses will now use lavish retirement plans to keep the best advisors and starve smaller advisors by reducing payouts and benefits.

Semi-Independents and Partnered Indies

Just as protocol is being dismantled in the wire house world, the independent model is also changing. The industry term is "bifurcating." It used to be that you simply set up your own firm and got your own vendors to support that firm. But now there are other models of being independent. Twenty years ago most of these other

34 "Destination RIA: What to Expect and How to Prepare for Independence," *Wealth Management*, https://www.wealthmanagement.com/resources/destination-ria-what-expect-and-how-prepare-independence.

options didn't exist. You were either with a wire house or you were 100 percent independent.

Semi-independents are the middle ground between a wire house and a pure independent. You find a lot of smaller advisors in these semi-independents because of the time it takes to operate one's own business. These advisors outsource their back-office functions—e.g., technology, compliance—in a similar way to how a wire house advisor outsources those functions to Merrill Lynch. It costs 10 to 20 percent of your revenue to have these functions provided for you (at around \$1–2 million in revenue). At the same time, these advisors have picked up independence because they have some autonomy in decision-making.

But semi-independents don't get the full advantage of being independent. You are still subject to someone else's platform. And if you want to leave that platform, it's similar to picking up your book of business and moving it to a wire house like Merrill Lynch or UBS. It's a pain. That's why you don't see too many larger advisors going semi-independent. On the other side, we are seeing more and more large teams/firms look for this option because of the things we have written about. If they can outsource all the back-office, they can focus on vision and growing the firm. Surprisingly, the cost for larger teams/firms is very appealing and can get down to four to ten basis points.

Partnered indies provide another option for an entrepreneurial advisor who wants to be independent, control their own decisions, and not be locked into someone else's platform but also needs some help because the whole picture of running a practice is too overwhelming. In the partnered indie space, our strong recommendation is to start by hiring an independent consultant who isn't trying to convince you of their model. There is simply no way for you to understand all the pluses and minuses without the guidance of somebody who has been there and done that having worked with these different options before. They will come in, get to know your firm, bring in finalists for your team to meet, and then handle all contract negotiations. Partnered indies have gone out and created platforms, but, in theory, they have chosen the best of the best, and you can customize it a little. They use their size to push down the costs of the platform vendors and can also help by consulting on other issues.

Aggregators have also stepped into this space. They provide a list of services to independent firms in exchange for equity or a percentage of revenue. The aggregators all have different styles. Without a consultant, it's mind-boggling to go through what each aggregator offers. You need somebody at your side who knows all these firms (for example, Focus Financial, PCG, Hightower, and United are all aggregators). Your consultant learns about your firm and guides you toward the right partner because there are so many options. Every aggregator has a different financial structure and operations style. Some may help best with operations, some may be best at helping you grow, and some may be best if you are in need of capital.

Fundamental Choice: Employee or Entrepreneur?

Wire houses have changed with the dismantling of protocol. Independents have changed to include semi-independents and partnered indies. An advisor's fundamental choice, however, remains the same: do you want to be an employee, or do you want to be an entrepreneur?

For the advisor who is stuck at $1–2 million in revenue and is trying to figure out how to get to the next level, that advisor's fundamental choice is the same today as it was twenty years ago: employee or entrepreneur? The Type A personalities reading this book will say, "There's no decision to be made—of course I want to be an entrepreneur."

But that's not true for everyone. Entrepreneurs often have a difficult time balancing life and work. There are many advisors out there who say, "I want to be an employee because it takes a lot of work off my back, which leaves me more time to play golf or go to my kid's baseball game."

The thing that we underestimated when we went independent—and that every single advisor we've met also underestimated when they went independent—was the amount of time you spend doing nonclient advising activities. In other words, it takes a ton of time and effort to run your own business. If you're not interested in making that kind of investment of time and energy, then staying at a wire house or working as an advisor for someone who will make those commitments is a prudent choice.

Benefits to Working at a Wire House

If you're not entrepreneurial in your mindset, then staying as an employee at a wire house is smart. And there are some important benefits to the wire house world.

The first benefit of working at a wire house is brand. When you call somebody or meet somebody whose business you're trying to get and you say, "I'm with Merrill Lynch," nobody says, "Who?" That brand often pays off more and more the bigger the account size you're seeking. We had prospective clients turn us down when we were independent because they only wanted to do business with a major wire house. They believed they would get better investment opportunities, and if something went wrong, the wire house would stand behind it. They just didn't have that same faith in our independent shop.

The next benefit to being at a wire house is that there's somebody else doing a lot of the work that most advisors don't want to do, like running the P/L, compliance, and technology—i.e., the infrastructure of your firm. Some advisors really get into that, but many don't;

they just want to work with clients. Not having to manage the infrastructure of your firm frees up time that you can spend looking for new business, envisioning your strategic plan at one year, three years, ten years, or twenty years, or finding the best investments, etc.

The third benefit to being at a wire house is you don't have employees. The wire house has employees. A wire house advisor may have eight people on his team, and he may pay for some of those people out of his own pocket, but they still aren't his employees. He doesn't have to deal with HR, retirement plans, bonus plans, or employee reviews; these are all handled by the wire house. That's a big time-saver because managing people is an enormous amount of work.

The fourth benefit is the advent of new retirement plans at many of the wire houses. This is a recent development. In the past, wire house retirement plans were so inferior to the market value of a good advisor's business that it wasn't even worth talking about. Today, however, a medium to large-size advisor can get two to two and a half times the gross revenue of their book of business at retirement paid over time. That's a good valuation for a retiring advisor that takes little effort.

The last benefit is annual income for advisors of a certain size. For those who break through the $1–2 million barrier and are doing $4–6 million and above, these advisors' gross incomes before personal expenses can get as high as 48 to 52 percent, including all deferred compensation. In order for your personal net income to exceed that as an independent, you have to become a large and successful independent. Not to say you can't exceed that (the good independents take home 65–70 percent of revenue), but you have to scale effectively, as we have discussed in earlier chapters, for your personal income to exceed what you could take home from a wire house—or you run an extremely lean shop from which you can't scale or deliver relationship alpha effectively.

Disadvantages to Working at a Wire House

There are certainly drawbacks to the wire house world. The most serious one is the inability to participate in the largest growth opportunity in the industry—M&A. This opportunity is going to be around for the next ten to twenty years, as older advisors are retiring and selling their businesses, but if you're at a wire house, you just can't participate in the same way.

That's not to say you can't participate at all. If you work at Merrill Lynch, you can certainly make a deal to buy another Merrill Lynch employee's book of business. But it's management's decision, not yours. So, while you do have some freedom to play the acquisitions game, if you're an advisor with Merrill Lynch, you can't acquire anyone who isn't a Merrill Lynch employee.

The second disadvantage is the lack of control in how you serve clients. You have little to no control over what software you're able to employ to find the right solution for your clients. You have limited control over what investment options can be brought to the table to serve your clients. You have limited control over which employees you use in your practice to serve your clients. We recall one time at UBS when we were told we couldn't hire an intern, let alone a full-time employee, even if we paid for it ourselves because of a corporate hiring freeze.

Another disadvantage is that brand can work against you. If a UBS advisor in Florida is prosecuted for tax evasion and the case makes headlines, that could affect an advisor in Colorado even though she had nothing to do with it. As a wire house advisor, you are associated with a big brand—and whatever that big brand is doing.

We've experienced this personally. When we were at Smith Barney, the firm came under attack from clients when a big insider trading case was on the front page of the *Wall Street Journal* almost daily. Then it happened again when UBS was involved in a tax evasion scandal involving offshore banking. Some of our bigger accounts came to us and said, "We just can't be associated with you right now." We were shocked, as it had nothing to do with us, but the clients were serious.

Finally—and this is a critical point that we'll talk about more below—if you are a large enough advisor, there's no way to monetize your life's work at the highest level if you stay at a wire house. You can simply sell your business for more money as an independent than you can at a wire house.

Benefits to Being Independent

We're talking here about pure independents—i.e., those who are not associated with another firm in any way. The core advantages of being independent are the flip side of the disadvantages to being a wire house advisor:

- The single biggest advantage to being independent is the ability to participate in the largest growth opportunity in the industry, M&A.
- The second benefit is the ability to make your own decisions. You decide what technology and what investment products your clients are going to use.
- The third benefit is not being associated with a wire house brand. There are people who despise the wire houses and will only do business with independents.
- The fourth core advantage is the ability to monetize your life's work at the highest valuation.

Another benefit of being independent is that after you retire, you can continue to draw an income stream from the company you built. There are many independent advisors who build a thriving brand, retire, and continue to profit from the business even though they're no longer advising clients. You can't do that at a wire house. When you retire, you have to leave the business completely.

Independent advisors also have the ability to control their working environment. We had a partner once who said to us, "If I'm going to spend sixteen hours a day working, I want to be in the space that I want to be in." Sometimes that means establishing your office near your home so you don't have to drive through traffic. Sometimes that means customizing the physical surroundings of the office—having a gym or a certain kind of furniture. You get to create your own environment, which is no small deal to advisors who work long hours.

Next is the ability to compensate employees with a piece of the pie, which we call "alignment." When you own your own firm and can give your team a piece of the action, it's much easier to align employees and get everybody moving in the same direction.

The final benefit is the tax effect. This is a huge advantage of being independent from an operating standpoint. When you are an employee of a wire house, your income gets taxed as ordinary income. When you own your own company, it can get taxed at a much lower rate. The spread between those two today is around 15 percent—i.e., when you monetize your book of business at a wire house, you'll be taxed more than if you monetize your own company by a similar percentage. If that's $20 million for half your business, you're paying $3 million extra in taxes as a wire house advisor.

Disadvantages to Being Independent

The greatest challenge to being independent is having to do everything that other people used to do for you. It was a huge surprise to us to learn how much time it takes to run an independent firm.

The P&L, compliance, technology, office space—all these things take enormous amounts of time. At our firm, which was doing $10 million in revenue, it took the vast majority of one partner's time just to deal with those issues, not to mention the support people underneath that person.

In other words, it took one owner running the business almost full-time—plus somebody running compliance, somebody running operations and HR, somebody running reporting, and somebody running accounting. Not many firms hire that many full-time employees, but the point is that those are areas *somebody* has to run. In a wire house, many of these are handled for you.

The next disadvantage is the challenge of establishing a brand. Most clients want their advisor to have a recognizable brand, and when you go independent you don't have a brand until you spend time and money building one. We call it "Who's your firm again?" because you get asked that a lot when you go independent.

The third disadvantage is there is no one but you if you get sued. A sad but true fact in our industry is the larger you get as an advisor the more likely you are to have some legal action brought against you. In most cases, this has nothing to do with the quality of the advisors; it has to do with our litigious society. There are many lawyers out there advertising, "Sue your financial advisor" every time the market goes down. Somebody will take advantage whenever there's a big, negative event in the market, so if you've been in the business long enough, it's going to happen.

This problem is exacerbated by the fact that insurance companies will settle almost anything for six figures. They do this because they've done the economic analysis, and it's cheaper to settle for $100K than it is to fight a lawsuit. Every advisor has malpractice insurance, so if you've got lawyers willing to go after it and insurance companies willing to pay, there are going to be lawsuits.

That our society is set up this way is a disadvantage to independents. A wire house is going to have a big law firm representing them, but in independent land, you're on the hook for lawyers' fees and the time it takes to go through the whole nightmare whether you're innocent or not.

The Economic Difference

If you're going to do all this extra work as an independent, there's got to be some advantage to it, right? The bottom line is a really well-run RIA should make 65–70 percent of revenue as earnings before owner's compensation (EBOC). Meaning, after you've paid off all your expenses but before you pay yourself as owner, you should make 65 percent of your gross earnings.

Most smaller RIAs in the $500K to $1 million revenue range will struggle to make 30 to 40 percent EBOC. The benchmarking studies from Fidelity and Schwab show that high-performing teams have between 60 and 70 percent EBOC—not just because they're better at running a business but because they've been successful at bringing in bigger clients and increasing the productivity of the team around them so that each relationship manager can handle a higher number of clients.

On the wire house side, the low end is about 35 percent of your gross earnings and the high end is 48 to 52 percent, and it's completely based on how much revenue you do. If you're going to be a $500,000 to $1 million advisor, or even if you're going to get stuck at $1.5 million, you will probably make just as much annual income at a wire house as you would being independent.

Most people don't believe that. Most people think the big advantage to going independent is that their income is going to rise dramatically. But they haven't had to run a P&L or been forced to understand all the expenses of running an independent shop. It's a big misconception that your income is automatically going to rise.

If you're going to be a larger advisor doing $2 million or $3 million or more in revenue, and you're willing to put in the extra workload, then you can certainly increase your annual compensation by being independent. But to be clear, this isn't triple or quadruple. This is the difference between 48 to 52 percent and 60 to 70 percent. Or said another way, if you're making $4 million in revenue, we're talking about a difference of 10 to 20 percent on that, or $400K to $800K a year.

If you're a larger advisor, don't go independent solely for the opportunity to make a slightly higher income. If you're doing $4 million in revenue and can take home half that, is making $2.6 million instead of $2 million worth it to take on all the extra work of being independent? Remember, you likely have a tax spread in addition to this. The reason you go independent is not solely the annual income—it's because of the economics that can happen by acquiring other firms and by monetizing your life's work. The reasons to go independent are controlling the decisions yourself and the ability to scale and monetize your life's work for the best valuation. M&A and monetization are huge advantages to being independent.

The reason you go independent is not solely the annual income—it's because of the economics that can happen by acquiring other firms and by monetizing your life's work.

We mentioned that many wire houses' new retirement plans pay between two to two and a half times gross revenue at retirement.

In the independent space, a firm's valuation is not priced on gross revenue; it's priced on EBOC. A larger firm will get between six and ten times that number.

An advisor doing $1.5 million in revenue will not benefit by going independent, neither in annual income nor at retirement. He or she would be better off staying at a wire house and retiring there. At the right wire house, his or her business's valuation at retirement might be as high as $3 million. If he or she were independent, that number would be similar, possibly even less. A $1.5 million advisor is probably taking home 45 percent, or $630K. Even four times that amount (an independent advisor with $1.5 million gross revenue can expect to get three to four times EBOC) is just over $2.5 million.

Your selling multiple keeps going up the more revenue you do. For example, the $1.5 million advisor above is doing great to get four times net earnings. If revenue is $4–5 million, you can get four and a half to five times. If you're in the $6–7 million range, you can get five and a half to six times. If you're in the $7 million range, you can get seven times. At $10 million, you might get eight to ten times. The key is growing your independent firm in size before you monetize your life's work.

Arbitraging the Multiple

As noted, the economic story of being independent is not so much about annual income. It's about being able to use M&A to drive the size of your firm, which then drives up the value of your company when you're ready to sell as well as your personal income as you grow.

The monetization amount is all dependent on the size of your firm. How do you grow most efficiently? It's not through traditional marketing—i.e., one client at a time. It's through M&A work. If you have a $10 million firm and buy an advisor doing $500K in revenue, you're buying at that advisor's selling multiple, which might be two or three. But when you sell that practice, you've rolled it into your bracket, which is a seven to ten times selling multiple. You bought for two to three times and are able to sell for seven to ten.

Take an independent firm doing $10 million in revenue with EBOC at 65 percent, or $6.5 million. To illustrate our point, eight times that amount is a $52 million valuation for the entire book of business. Half of that means you're selling half your practice for well over $20 million.

CHAPTER 11
HOW TO MAKE A GRACEFUL EXIT

Have you ever had a great weekend, figured out some important things about family and life, and felt fresh and revitalized on Sunday? You wake up on Monday filled with excitement and are ready to go to work only to see that conviction completely reversed by Tuesday.

If you feel this way, then it's time to change what you're doing—perhaps to the models discussed in this book—or look for a graceful exit. A graceful exit is one that honors your clients, your employees, and your partners. It's also one that allows you to feel blessed by the people and the process and lucky to have had this chance in life. How do you create that kind of exit?

Step One: Financial Readiness, Maximized Valuation, Emotional Readiness

Financial readiness. First, you must have your firm financially prepared for your exit. This one is very straightforward: You need to figure out if you sell for *x* price that, after you pay taxes and expenses, you have enough net money to invest and live comfortably for the rest of your life. Further, your firm's finances should be prepared with an EBOC standard going back three years, identifying any issues like client concentration, age, complaints, etc.

Maximized valuation. Second, you need to have checked off all the boxes we talk about in this book because having your team and systems in place is going to maximize your value. Most importantly, you've got to have relationship managers in place so that a buyer can look at your firm and understand how it will continue to operate when you are no longer there. The buyer will see that the clients aren't vested in the exiting senior advisor but rather the relationship managers.

To maximize valuation, you also need to have all of your systems in place. Your operational structure must be set up so it's easy to manage client relationships. Your asset management must be set up so you're managing model portfolios. Some firms are still stuck in the days where, if they change from investment A to B, they need to go through each client one by one to figure out exactly how they will adjust. It's very difficult to attract a buyer if that's the case because it's impossible to scale a firm like that. You also need thorough client records that show you're in contact and know the needs of each—i.e., what their performance has been and what their goals are.

Most importantly, you've got to have relationship managers in place so that a buyer can look at your firm and understand how it will continue to operate when you are no longer there.

A great measurement of readiness is knowing where your firm is weak. Maybe you don't have a trading system in place, so you're still managing all accounts individually. That's going to hurt your valuation. Or maybe you acknowledge that last year you brought in five new relationships and lost ten. This measurement is instructive because it lets you know where you need to improve to maximize valuation, and it lets you know if you're really ready to sell. You will come to stark realizations.

Either you are or are not willing to correct client retention by getting back out there and increasing your client contact from two meetings a year to four. Either you are or are not willing to do seminars and advertising and spend the money and time to add more accounts. Either you are or are not willing to invest the money to put software and people in place and have the right infrastructure for maximizing the valuation of your firm. Put simply, firms that are growing consistently are worth more than firms that are not growing or losing assets.

If you look in the mirror and realize you aren't willing to do those things to correct the problems, then you've taken the firm as far as you can, and it's probably time for you to go.

A great way to find where you're weak is to have an outside consultant come in and act like a buyer. Those of us who have done M&A can quickly identify the problems and show you solutions. Then, when you're ready to sell, the real buyers won't see those issues—or, at the minimum, you can turn those issues from problems into opportunities when speaking with a buyer. The real point is if the buyer finds the problem, it will hurt your valuation; if you present the problem as "why you are seeking the right buyer," then can turn a negative into a positive.

Emotional readiness. A mistake a lot of advisors make is they think it's time to go when they feel burnt out. Just because you feel exhausted and unmotivated is not a good reason to look to sell your business, and it's really important that advisors realize this. The problem with using burnout as a reason to sell is that we *all* feel like this many times in our careers. We've talked in this book about what you do to recover from burnout—put a team around you, keep yourself in good physical shape, devote time to your family, consider sabbaticals, and utilize your faith or belief system. But most important is to have a plan so you can see the light at the end of the tunnel.

It's important that you don't sell simply because you're burned out and think the grass is greener on the other side. An advisor might be saying, "I'll just sell and take on the next chapter of life." Retirement doesn't come without challenges as well. You make a decision to sell when you're not willing to take the firm to the next level or because you've checked all the boxes and reached the highest valuation you're going to reach.

You make a decision to sell when you're not willing to take the firm to the next level or because you've checked all the boxes and reached the highest valuation you're going to reach.

The best reason we've ever heard to sell is when the advisor believes they have taken the firm as far as they can, and it's time for someone else to lead. They've run their firm like we've outlined in this book. But they just simply don't have the educational background or capabilities to move their client base from where they are in revenue to $10 million or more. They haven't developed the necessary niche, and they're at a point in their lives where they're not going to. They look at their world and make an honest assessment: "I've taken this as far as I can. It's time for the next level of leadership to come in and lead."

Step Two: Infrastructure Setup for the Transition

First, you need to convert all your clients to fee-based revenue. There are two ways to get paid in our industry: fees (charging a certain percentage of assets under management) and commission (earned by selling certain products). No one is going to buy the commission-based revenue because it's not repeatable revenue. Buyers only buy fee-based revenues.

Second, you need to show that your team is meeting with clients regularly. That could be twice a year or four times a year, depending on your firm. Regardless, it's really important that the buyer knows these relationships are in good standing.

Third, you have to make yourself irrelevant. Whether you call them relationship managers, senior vice presidents, or partners, what's important is that the client relationships are vested in other people, not you. If you haven't put relationship managers in place and you are personally still integral to some clients being at the firm, then the buyer is going to discount what they're willing to pay. They're assuming some of these clients will leave when you leave. Or they'll say, "You can't leave. We'll pay you a consulting fee to keep these clients here." That's a new expense to the firm that lowers net income and will lower the multiple on that income that you can get for selling.

Fourth, you build presence in other members of the firm. We didn't do this one well, but we learned from that mistake. "Presence" means an advisor a client can look up and see that the advisor is a subject matter expert. We've touched on some of the many ways you get presence, like publishing articles, giving speeches, and getting further education. When the senior advisor and subject matter expert is leaving, the clients need to feel like there are other experts ready to fill those shoes.

Fifth, you need to be operationally self-sufficient, which means the trading system, the CRM, and proper P/L statements and financial statements for your firm. This also means eliminating liabilities and contingent liabilities. A big mistake sellers make is leaving personal loans to the company on the books. Most every business owner loans money to their business from time to time. If you have loaned money to your company, get it paid back before you sell. You won't get it paid back in a sale because the buyer will treat it as equity. Another mistake sellers make is creating contingent liabilities. Long-term leases are the classic example. Be sure all your leases are short-term so a buyer isn't locked in. If that buyer wants to pick up your business and move it to a different location, he or she is not saddled with that liability. Again, having an outside consultant is important to correcting these mistakes now, before pursuing a sale.

Finally, you need to align key employees. Imagine being a buyer thinking about buying a firm but the only advisor you're able to talk to is the one who wants to sell his or her interest in the firm. That buyer doesn't know the relationship managers or how strong their relationships are with clients. Yet many sellers don't want a buyer talking to their employees because they don't want those employees to know that they're selling. You must get past this mindset, which means making key employees part of the selling process. This entails talking to them about what you're doing and why you're doing it. It means aligning their pay structure and giving them part of the sale. If you don't get your key relationship managers and your operations manager on board, you're never going to get the maximum valuation.

Step Three: Your Story Creates Stability

You need to have a clear and concise story about why you're selling the firm. A buyer does not want to hear that you're selling in order to get rich. They understand that component of it, but there also has to be a story explaining why you're taking this step.

For example, when we were selling our firm, our story was that we had had our relationship managers with us for a long time—fourteen years on average—and it was time that they got a shot at the golden ring. It was time for them to be owners of the company.

Part of it was us cashing out, of course. But the more important part of the story was our relationship managers were being given the opportunity to take control of the firm. A buyer could understand that. In fact, they could really get their arms around the deal and get excited about it because the story showed that the people taking over leadership were long-standing, trustworthy, successful advisors.

Another example of a well-defined story is "I've taken this company as far as I know how to take it. I need knowledge above me to take it to the next level." Buyers need to perceive that kind of integrity coming from the seller so they don't feel like they're getting taken.

Part of your story is why you're selling the firm; another part is encouraging the buyer to see the upside. Every selling firm needs to look at what the benefit is for the buyer. You have to create what we call "blue sky," which answers the question, what's the upside for the buyer in purchasing this company? Where can they take it that it hasn't been before?

When we were selling our company, for example, the blue sky was more mergers and acquisitions. We had situated the firm to continue pursuing M&A deals. We had relationship managers (with capacity) and operational systems and asset management all in place. We had done multiple M&A deals before, so the firm was in the position to continue growing that way. The firm that bought us considered themselves experts in M&A work and could easily see that we were a base they could use to acquire around us.

Another upside for the buyer could be the possibility of increasing services and fees. The buyer may look at the selling firm and decide that there are additional revenue opportunities by offering more services or going after untapped areas. A great example is a seller who has a book of business owners but doesn't do retirement plans or P/C insurance. There are lots of new revenue possibilities. Or you may be able to show the buyer how their lower operational costs will affect profitability. If you're selling to a large buyer, their operational costs will be minute compared to yours. If you're making 45 percent EBOC, that buyer could make 60 percent because their custodial cost is four basis points while yours is fifteen. We bought a firm, for example, where those were the numbers. Our cost was four basis points to provide all the custody and trading. The firm we bought was paying fifteen basis points. Eleven basis points on $100 million adds up to a lot of money.

Buyers Evaluate Risk, Not Reward

What do buyers want, and how do you provide it? All buyers evaluate risk, not reward. They're all looking for what could go wrong with the acquisition; they're not nearly as worried about what they'll make with the acquisition. Of course, they look at the net income they'll pick up, but they take that as a given—and they have a model that will tell them how many years it will take them to pay for the transaction. More important is the risk. What they're looking for is "How does this thing go wrong?" If you understand that, you can be better prepared to monetize your business.

***

Answer these questions *before* you ever meet a buyer:

Why Won't Clients Leave?

The answer has to be because they're vested in the relationship managers. But this should go beyond the RMs. You want to have a really solid answer for why—when this iconic figure who started the firm leaves—that some clients aren't also going to leave. If you tell the buyer that you're willing to take an earn-out and receive money over a number of years instead of up front, then the buyer will see that you are confident in clients staying (because you won't get paid if they don't). Additionally, if you explain to the buyer all the relationship alpha things your RMs are doing for clients—that your firm has become the quarterback at the center of clients' financial lives—then that buyer is going to see that those clients are heavily embedded in your firm.

Why Won't Key Personnel Leave?

You need to assure the buyer that the key RMs and operations manager are going to stay. Just because they bought into the sale does not mean that they'll stick around after the transition. Why won't they go work for a competitor? You need to show the buyer that in the new firm structure, these crucial personnel are receiving ongoing compensation. Using an earn-out model for some of that ongoing compensation also works with key personnel because it shows the buyer that these folks have to stay in order to get paid. Another way to demonstrate that personnel won't leave is encouraging the buyer to include them in the new ownership structure. Finally, you can use employment contracts. Go to these personnel and say, "I want to make sure you're protected in this transaction. Here's a five-year employment contract with the new firm."

What Are You Doing about Infrastructure Holes?

If you have holes in your infrastructure, like an outdated trading system, you better be able to tell the buyer how you're going to solve that problem for them. You need to have set up outsourced solutions to fill those holes. A classic example of an infrastructure hole is not having thorough client records that detail every piece of paper a client needs to be invested. That particular hole can create legal exposure, so it's something that you just need to solve—or don't sell your company.

What's the Portfolio Management Risk?

You must be able to sit down with a buyer and say, "Here's how we manage money, this is why it's worked well, and here's some proof that we've had decent returns." To be clear, your portfolios do *not* need to be the No. 1 performing portfolios in the world, but you better be able to show that they aren't the worst performing either because the buyer will figure that out. Buyers go through and look at what various clients have made on their assets, so consistent returns, based on client objectives, are also important. If your portfolios aren't as strong as you'd like them to be, you need to address that up front with integrity: "Asset management is not our greatest strength, so one of the things we're looking for in a buyer is one that has great asset management. We'll talk to clients about your asset management."

What's the Transition Risk?

It's essential to lay out for the buyer how you're going to transition clients from your firm to the buyer's firm. Don't wait for them to tell you. Let them know exactly how it's going to happen and how it's not going to change the buyer's entire way of life to onboard hundreds of new accounts. Explain that your RMs are rock-solid in these relationships, and they will continue to run these accounts. If the seller is really sharp, he or she will show the buyer how the transition will be introduced to clients—for example, personal visits for the top 10 percent of clients, phone calls for next 20 percent, and letters for the remaining 70 percent. This shows the buyer there's a well-thought-out plan in place for making a smooth transition.

What's the Legal Risk?

If you don't have a clean legal background—i.e., if you've ever been sued—you better have all the details written up. You need to explain to the buyer exactly what happened and exactly why this isn't an issue in your business moving forward. Write out who paid the settlement and whether or not you participated. Having been sued is not a deal breaker for a buyer. We live in a litigious society, and most advisors who have been around as long as we have eventually get sued. You also need to have a compliance manual that shows how you're mitigating legal risk. This is a formal, written document. And lastly, if you're really on top of your game, you can do a compliance audit that shows there are no big legal risks in your firm.

***

There are many firms that sell without having all of these questions answered up front.

Why? They don't understand the risks and don't know that they are leaving money on the table. If you can't answer each of the above questions, that will create doubt in the buyer's mind. A seller's failure to understand that will result in the buyer taking a turn, or half turn, or quarter turn off the sale price. Where x is the selling firm's net income, instead of the buyer paying $4x$, they'll pay $3.75x$, $3.5x$, or even less.

What If Selling Doesn't Feel Right? Other Options for Monetizing

If you're ready to move on but selling doesn't seem like the right decision, what are your other options for making a graceful exit?

Transition ownership to key staff members. This is done often for two main reasons: 1) people want to reward the employees who've helped them build the business, and 2) it's the easiest way. If you transition to key staff members, you don't have to merge two organizations or explain to clients that you're selling the firm. The advantages are the ease and reduction in risk. If you decide to go this way, it's important for you to get a majority of the profits and *not have to continue working*, which means you may need to hire additional people so you can truly stop working.

There are three main disadvantages to transitioning ownership to key staff members. The first is the valuation won't be your highest, meaning you could probably get more from a third party than you could from internal staff. Your staff members are not professional buyers of companies, and there are no synergy savings from a buyer who has a similar operation.

The second reason can come as a shock. Many advisors who choose to sell their company to their staff have to keep working during the transition. For example, say a firm is generating $2 million in revenue and putting 50 percent to the bottom line. That senior advisor is making $1 million, and he or she decides to sell the company to team members for five times that amount, or $5 million. The team would keep doing what they've been doing and pay that senior advisor $1 million annually over five years. In theory, that senior advisor would not work during that time. In practice, that rarely happens.

When there is no new blood at the table—versus bringing in an outside, third-party buyer—the seller ends up having to continue working. Why? The seller wants to make sure he or she gets that $1 million a year, and there's nothing forcing him or her to fully detach from the firm. A new owner provides the motivation for the seller to detach, but only if the seller's role is adequately replaced. For example, we find that many sellers are the lead asset gatherers. When they sell, the firm loses its main new client funnel. As a result, the business does not do well after the sale. The seller then has to keep working in order to keep the firm doing well enough to pay the seller his or her annual earn-out.

We consulted with a firm owner who wanted to transition his ownership to key staff members. This senior advisor had followed everything in this book except he was still managing his firm's top twenty clients himself instead of using a relationship manager. The problem was none of his RMs were qualified to handle those top twenty accounts. During the transition, the senior advisor tried to get his RMs to do more of the work with those clients, yet they didn't have the skillset, so he was still doing the work. Guess what? This became five more years of work!

The third disadvantage is that legal risks are still with you. You're still the owner of the firm during the five-year, earn-out period. If you pursue this exit strategy over selling to a third party, it's essential to make sure you put together a structure where the net income of the business comes to you—but only after you truly stop working. When you stop working, you reduce legal exposure. We call that becoming "of counsel." In other words, you're there to advise the new owners but not work with clients.

Transition key roles but maintain ownership. This is similar to the first option except you remain an owner. It's a smarter option than many advisors might think. The owner goes out and hires a fixed-salary, C-level position (either a chief investment officer or a chief executive officer) to run the firm—i.e., to fill whatever the role the senior advisor was filling. That senior advisor can then step away from the firm while being able to ensure clients that the firm is in great shape with this new person involved. The senior advisor then keeps collecting dividend income forever.

Some refer to this as the "unlimited x deal" because if it works, you're basically selling your company in perpetuity. You're getting that net income forever. You can go ten years, for example, and get the same profitability each year: where *x* is your annual profit, you end up with *10x* instead of selling your business for *4x* or 5*x*.

Many business owners have done this outside of our industry—far less have done it within financial services. Outside of our industry, clients are less dependent on the business's owner. For example, if you own a company that makes coffee cups, you probably don't have a direct relationship with your customers. A financial advisor does.

But if you set up your company the right way—if you follow this book and all your client relationships are vested in your RMs and your structure is in place—then this is a possibility, and it's real. All you do is replace yourself and your functions with a C-level executive, which is not hard to find in the industry, and then step away and keep creating that net income forever.

Which firms should consider this option? Firms that are larger and well established. Firms that have high net income and high profitability. Firms that have their structure set up with RMs handling all of the client relationships. Firms where the owner can make himself or herself irrelevant. For those types of firms, this is a really good option for monetizing your life's work.

Of course, there are also disadvantages. You relinquish control without getting anything at the start. This means that if the people you handed over the firm to screw it up, it's going to be very hard for you to monetize later. Try selling a firm that's having problems—you're going to take a real hit on valuation. For that $2 million firm with 50 percent profitability, let's say that senior advisor uses half of his $1 million to hire his replacement, which means he now has $500K of profitability that first year. Meanwhile, the total book of business declines $500K because the senior advisor left, and those in charge haven't done a good job. Now that senior advisor is not getting any net income.

A buyer will see that business is going down, not up, and your valuation will be greatly reduced. The lesson here is that you must have supreme confidence in the people you're leaving to run the firm. If you don't and they mess things up, you could put yourself in a difficult position to monetize your life's work.

> **The lesson here is that you must have supreme confidence in the people you're leaving to run the firm. If you don't and they mess things up, you could put yourself in a difficult position to monetize your life's work.**

Partial sales, or the aggregator model. This is what we did. We sold half our company to an aggregator, which buys up partial interests in financial services firms. Focus Financial, PCG, and Dynasty are all examples of aggregators. The partial sale, using an aggregator, is a good solution to monetizing if you want a hybrid between these different options—especially if you don't own the entire firm.

The first advantage to a partial sale is that an aggregator will probably pay you one of the highest prices in the marketplace. Second, an aggregator usually comes in with skills to help the people who are now running the firm. Aggregators usually have different areas of specialty. For example, Focus Financial does a lot of work helping firms grow through M&A. Dynasty has an operational consulting platform to help you make sure you scale your business the right way. Third, most aggregators will give the next generation of ownership equity in the business. In other words, the aggregator buys 50 percent of the company—that's how the owner cashes out—and this allows you to sell the other 50 percent to key employees at a lower rate since you got the big check from the aggregator. This way you've honored the people who helped you build the business, you've created a system where the people who are left have some knowledge when things get difficult, and you've received a maximum valuation.

As always, there are disadvantages. A partial sales model can look really enticing, but there are many catches. For example, aggregators are often going to want a preferred return on what they paid you before the firm's remaining partners participate. With the complexity involved in partial deals, it's critical that you use a consultant to evaluate this and market your firm. The time it took us to learn this was nearly two years of our lives. You need to focus on keeping the business running well and use consultants who have actually had a business like yours and sold firms like these to prepare all the analyses for you to make good decisions with.

Timing Matters—Don't Let the Cycle Control You!

A lot of advisors are wondering, "Is this the right time to sell my business?" We live in economic cycles, so procrastinating too much can be problematic if a downturn is looming. Let's go back to how things looked in 2007. If you wanted to sell then, you would've needed to stay in the business for four to six more years to get the same valuations that were there in 2006–07. The problem today is that many of these advisors who are thinking about selling don't have four to six more years. They're tired.

The point is to be extremely aware of economic cycles. You need to realize when you're in a good market and your earnings are up. This is the time for you. If you're going to seek a sale in the next five years, do it now because you may not be able to control the future. If the future goes the other way, the cycle will control you.

When the cycle begins to control you, most of the firms we've seen decline rapidly. The mixture of a down cycle with a tired advisor can be an ugly combination. Most of these firms never get back to where they were. We're not saying that other firms don't rebound after a down cycle; firms that are younger and hungrier and in growth mode do come back. But if you're thinking about selling, you're in the downhill phase of your career. Getting geared up again to go big is really difficult for people who are in this exit mindset—and they never get back to where they were.

The message is if you're thinking about selling now, get on that decision. Make it once and for all, or be committed to staying for at least another four to six years.

If you're thinking about selling, you're in the downhill phase of your career. Getting geared up again to go big is really difficult for people who are in this exit mindset—and they never get back to where they were.

Leaving Your Staff and Clients in Good Hands

One of the most emotional things for a seller is leaving the staff and the clients who have become good friends. If you drop them in the wrong way, it will come back to haunt you. Let's start with how you leave your staff. If you haven't done everything you possibly could to protect the staff in this transaction and prepare them for what's going to happen—as well as let them know they were highly valued in your life—if things go badly after you sell, dealing with those people will take a huge toll on you.

Our advice is to give key staff members a chance to participate in the monetization. Before you say no to this, realize that big money to them is so much different than big money to you. If you're going to sell half your firm for $20 million, and you have four staff members for whom you'd double their salary as a bonus for the transaction, that's probably $400K. It's not even measurable in what you're receiving. Yet, to them, it's a gigantic bonus. Not only is it the right thing to do, it will also get them to stay positive with the buyer instead of being a problem.

Our other advice when it comes to staff is to communicate your plan and listen to what they want for their own careers. Tell them in advance—not after you've cut the deal. Many advisors are scared of telling their staff members because they think everyone is going to run out the door. They might, but the alternative is having to live with not telling them. If you've had someone with you for ten or twenty years and you don't trust them enough to share your plans, that's a problem.

You can turn this into a positive conversation. Tell them about your plan and then ask, "What do you want for the next stage of your career? Do you want to be here, or do you not want to be here? Do you want to be an owner, or do you not want to be an owner? Do you want to have this position or a different position?" If you make it about them, it becomes a positive conversation instead of a negative one.

As for your clients, you leave them in good hands by making sure they get a win in any transaction. We talked earlier about the massive reduction in cost when a smaller firm is bought by a larger firm—say, from fifteen basis points paid to the custodian down to four. Make sure in your deal that clients get some of that reduction in cost, or they get a much better reporting package, etc. Whatever it is, it has to be something that truly benefits them so you can say, "The new ownership has made opportunities available to our clients like … "

Failure to plan for leaving your staff and clients in good hands could mean leaving your life's work without so much as a thank you, much of your staff getting dismissed, and the model you built drastically changing. As always in this book, we're teaching from mistakes. We didn't do all of these things well, and we're still paying the price today. We wish we could have some of these back. We sold our firm, and there's basically no one still there other than the relationship managers. Regrettably, we don't feel like we protected them very well, and we're sure they don't feel great about us either.

If you do these things incorrectly, it could mean that you leave the work you've spent your career building with a whole bunch of bad feelings. We don't want you to make that mistake even though you started with great intentions.

CHAPTER 12
WHAT IS THE FUTURE?

What you think you know today will be very different later in your career. The advisor who is at the $1–2 million wall is going to see major changes in our industry.

When we were at that wall years ago, RIAs were practically nonexistent. If you weren't at one of the three or four big firms, you couldn't be an advisor on a large scale. Fast forward to today, and that picture has changed completely: many independent advisors have become more successful than any wire house advisor. Another example of change is managing money through models—this is a key to scaling the asset management side of your business—which didn't exist when we were at the $1–2 million wall. Today, it's *ho-hum*, so commonplace. Everybody does it.

Things have happened that were unthinkable twenty years ago. It's vital for today's advisors to realize that same type and speed of innovation is going to happen over the next few decades. Therefore, the advisor who is successful in the future will never stop learning, never stop evolving. In the words of the great Wayne Gretzky, "Skate to where the puck is going to be, not where it has been."

With over thirty years serving ultrahigh net worth clients, we believe the puck is moving toward advisors being the center of clients' financial lives—providing the relationship alpha services we've talked about in this book. The advisor of the future knows what clients care about and what keeps them awake at night. These services become indispensable. Clients couldn't imagine *not* having them. Whether that is access to advice about health care, budgeting/bill pay services, managing P/C insurance, working with families on transitional wealth, vetting unusual business opportunities, career planning for clients' children, etc. (see full list of relationship alpha services in Chapter 4), it has to be more than financial planning. Yes, this will require more work. It will require the team structure we have laid out. But, if done well, it will protect you from fee erosion and become what separates you from other advisors.

The advisor of the future knows what clients care about and what keeps them awake at night.

The 4th Revolution

If you're reading this and think the financial services industry isn't going to change that much—perhaps you think the evolution has already happened—consider how technology has upended entire industries over the last twenty years. In 1998, Kodak had 170,000 employees and sold 85 percent of all photo paper worldwide. Within just a few years, their business model disappeared, and they went bankrupt. In 1998, did you think that by the early 2000s you would never again take photos on film?

In the next five to ten years, software will continue to disrupt most traditional industries. Uber and Airbnb are data and information companies that specialize in logistics; neither own any cars or houses or hotels, yet they are the biggest taxi company and hospitality company in the world. Artificial intelligence is soaring, with computers becoming exponentially better at understanding the world we live in. IBM Watson can give legal advice within seconds and with 90 percent accuracy, compared to 70 percent for humans. AI is ushering in profound changes to the way law and medicine are practiced today, and it will have a huge impact in financial services as well.

Autonomous cars will alter the entire automobile industry. People who live in metropolitan areas won't own a car any longer; you'll call a car with your phone, and it will pick you up and drop you off—all without human drivers. The car insurance business model will disappear. Yes, disappear. What does this mean for the Allstates and Progressives of the world? Traditional car companies will try to evolve, while innovative companies like Tesla, Apple, and Google are taking the revolutionary approach and building computers on wheels that are connected to the Cloud.

The price of the cheapest 3-D printer went from $18K to $400 in ten years. In China and Dubai, companies have 3-D printed entire office buildings, pushing construction boundaries further. Human longevity is also changing drastically. The average life span is increasing three months per year; by 2070, life expectancy may increase to 150 years, according to CGTN.[35] What will this do for companies in health care?

Welcome to the fourth industrial revolution. Now try telling us that this reality *isn't* going to change financial advising. With the ease and sophistication of technology, we live in a world where clients are demanding more for the fees they pay. This reality is this will change the future of our business.

The successful advisor of the future will do more for clients than just financial planning and money management. The advisors who

---

35 "Human's Life Expectancy Can Reach 150, Say Experts," *CGTN*, October 11, 2017, https://news.cgtn.com/news/79516a4e7a597a6333566d54/share_p.html.

The successful advisor of the future will do more for clients than just financial planning and money management.

are doing this today have all worked to become recognized experts in their niche. All offer more services under one fee. All have focused their services around the demographic trends of an aging America and what these clients are looking for—supporting their lifestyle rather than growing capital, handling health care, and mitigating risk. These practices will structure their companies with fixed advisor salaries, enabling them to scale while still delivering high-end relationship alpha services. They will know where they are going because they have well-thought-out value statements, marketing plans, and business plans to support that growth.

Predictions for the Future

Solving the Age and Training Gap—Apprentice and Degree Programs

Our industry went through difficult years in the early 2000s. Between 2000 and 2012, the stock market had a zero rate of return. The banks, brokerages, and RIAs were all struggling to make money. As a result, things got cut. The industry stopped investing in training and recruiting.

Today, there's a gap in training and experience between advisors in their fifties and sixties and those in their thirties and forties. The gap has created a problem in advisor quality, but, perhaps more importantly, it has also created an opportunity for the thirty and forty-year-olds to buy the businesses of older advisors—as long as there are enough of those younger advisors out there. In 2017, *Forbes* noted that 38 percent of advisors are expected to retire in the next ten years while just 10 percent of current advisors are under the age of thirty-five.[36] A study by Cerulli Associates found that "for every eight advisors leaving the profession, only three new advisors are ready to take their place."[37]

The future is going to change how we recruit and train advisors. The industry is recognizing that it has to do a better job. The problems you read about in the news—the bad advisors, the blowups—are the result of the lack of training. Education is becoming a priority: 102 schools are listed in *Financial Planning*'s latest annual roundup of CFP Board-registered degree programs.[38] Our belief is that we'll also start seeing formal apprentice programs where younger advisors will have to work for older, more established advisors and become part of a team before they get to manage large clients and own a business.

Formal education is also going to change. Ten years from now, investment management is going to be a degree program at most major universities—just like accounting, economics, and business management. This is due to the fact that client demographics are changing dramatically: the number of Americans over the age of sixty-five is going to double by 2060 to over 98 million,[39] which means there will be increasing numbers of people in retirement in need investment management. Job growth will come from that area, and degree programs will pop up because they will be desperately needed.

---

36 Halah Touryalai, "America's Next Top-Gen Wealth Advisors: Millennials Who Survived 2008 are Now Managing Billions," *Forbes*, July 25, 2017, https://www.forbes.com/sites/halahtouryalai/2017/07/25/americas-next-gen-wealth-advisors-millennials-who-survived-2008-are-now-managing-billions/.

37 James J. Green, "The Changing Demographics of Advisors," *ThinkAdvisor*, September 28, 2015, https://www.thinkadvisor.com/2015/09/28/the-changing-demographics-of-advisors/.

38 Maddy Perkins, "102 Schools for Financial Planning," *Financial Planning*, October 1, 2018, https://www.financial-planning.com/list/colleges-for-financial-planning.

39 Mark Mather, "Fact Sheet: Aging in the United States," *Population Reference Bureau*, January 13, 2016, https://www.prb.org/aging-unitedstates-fact-sheet/.

Wire Houses Move to Salary-Bonus Model; Less Advisor Independence

The wire house world in the US still exists on a commission model. In other words, advisors get a piece of what clients pay the firm for investment advice. If you go to Europe, however, as we did to work for United Bank of Switzerland, you'll find that advisors there all get a salary with a bonus based on the assets they're managing and their client retention. There's a reason why operations at wire houses in Europe are far more profitable than operations at wire houses in the US. They control their cost of labor.

Twenty years from now, wire houses in the US are going to look a lot different. First, their advisors will be on this salary-bonus model. Second, most of the investment solutions they use will be generated by the bank they work for—versus today, where a hallmark of financial consulting is your independence and your ability to select the best investment managers in the world. The hallmark of the wire house advisor twenty years from now is going to be *what bank do you work for and what great products and services do they offer?* The advisors who don't like that—and a whole bunch aren't going to enjoy being limited in that way—will go independent so they'll have more choices.

The wire houses will end up competing with RIAs by offering a full package of lending, accounting, and asset management to the client, something RIAs can't offer. J. P. Morgan is already doing this. In other words, wire houses will become a one-stop shop for all your financial needs. If you need to borrow money for your business, you get it there. If you need to do your tax return, you get it there. If you need your assets managed, you get it there. The wires will use their lending power to drive that relationship.

Advisors will choose where they want to be—wire house or RIA—based on lifestyle. Those who are okay with solutions being created by the company they work for and any who are okay being an employee will work for wire houses. Those who aren't okay with that will go the independent route to seek higher income by doing all the things we've talked about in this book. But don't be fooled. What the wire house will be creating is the relationship alpha we have talked about.

Emergence of the Super Regional RIA

Today, we have the wire houses and the independents. Some of those independents are going to become aggressive acquirers. Ultimately, they'll acquire enough RIAs so that they become major players in their regions. This is another way of saying that consolidation is going to continue in the industry, but that consolidation is going to create super-regional independent firms that become well known in the areas they serve. And because these super-regional brand names will become so influential, the big banks and wire houses will end up having to buy the super regionals just to compete.[40] Further, they will pay more for them.

Fee Compression Will Continue and How to Avoid It

Some believe that fee compression won't happen on the advisor's side—it will only happen on the asset manager's side. They would be wrong because fee compression will continue on both sides. So asset managers better figure out how to make money at forty basis points or less, and advisors must figure out how to do more work to maintain their fees and their relationship alpha services.

The advisor of the future will be constantly pressed to keep existing clients happy or acquire new clients with fee compression driving clients to cheaper options. The consumer of financial services

40 Mindy Diamond, "The New Buyers: Familiar Names with Deep Pockets," *Diamond Consultants*, June 29, 2018, https://www.diamond-consultants.com/the-new-buyers-familiar-names-with-deep-pockets/.

reads article after article and sees commercial after commercial from custodians and low-cost fund providers telling them about how low their fees are. This is something clients understand. They may not understand risk-adjusted returns or how low correlations protect portfolios in down markets, but they understand fees. The more technology evolves, the more the client will see moving to a low-cost solution as a viable option.

The only way an advisor maintains price integrity is by doing more for the client. You would probably be willing to pay your personal CPA more if he also did your budget and paid your bills. Likewise, clients are willing to pay their advisor more for additional services. The successful advisor of the future keeps clients and avoids fee compression by doing more for the same dollars being earned today. You don't have to discount your fees if you become the center of the client's life. These advisors will, in turn, push down other vendor costs from custodians to software providers to be able to staff correctly to maintain these new services.

Relationship Alpha Gains Importance

The advisor of the future is more of a life coach than an asset manager. He or she is the quarterback of the client's financial life, bringing relationship alpha as much as investment alpha. Schwab's RIA Benchmarking Study notes, "Nearly half (41 percent) of advisors say the independent model will differentiate most significantly from captive models by offering clients

The advisor of the future is more of a life coach than an asset manager. He or she is the quarterback of the client's financial life, bringing relationship alpha as much as investment alpha.

a broad range of services—such as tax planning, charitable planning, and health care planning—that fall outside the realm of traditional portfolio management."[41]

The study continues, saying that 44 percent of advisors are providing more services to their clients without charging for them, and 40 percent have been putting more time into each client without increasing fees. The advisor of the future constantly thinks about how to add value to the client's life—even such things as helping older clients, who are challenged by technology, find helpful smartphone apps that allow them to enjoy life more.[42] By delivering this level of service, the advisor of the future earns the right to ask for referrals and avoids the fee compression happening in the industry. We will always recall the wise words of Consulting Group's CEO Frank Campanale: "Price is only an issue in the absence of value … so where's your value?"

Although it's still the viewpoint in much of the industry, we can no longer be only investment consultants. By helping clients solve health care needs, advise children on career opportunities, evaluate how to maximize the value of their business, and do budgeting and bill pay shows that you have a different, more important role in the client's life. As a result of these services, client meetings changed when we started doing those things at our firm. When we started providing relationship alpha, we talked less and less about performance and more and more about what was going on in their life.

Today, managing health care is a key relationship alpha service. Since more and more of these big clients are not working in traditional jobs and don't get health care through their employer, a critical

---

41 "2017 RIA Benchmarking Study," *Charles Schwab.*

42 Joseph F. Coughlin, "Uber Has Changed the World. Now it's Changing Aging, Too," accessed November 21, 2018, https://www.hartfordfunds.com/ad/uber-has-changed-the-world.html.

issue becomes accessing top quality health care and paying for it. Most ultrahigh net worth clients hate paying insurance premiums and hate filing for reimbursements even more. Most can afford to self-insure up to a certain level. A great advisor can determine if a client can afford to self-insure for $10K–20K a year. They then help the client find a high deductible insurance plan to reduce catastrophic risk and marry that to a high-end medical concierge service so the family can always have the best care. Note that we're not saying the advisor of the future will be an insurance agent. He or she will simply coordinate services through partnerships with people who specialize with each area that the advisor has found and researched.

The advisor of the future becomes the solution to what clients are worrying about. The ultrahigh net worth investor, who is part of America's aging demographic, is more focused on their children and grandchildren than themselves. The advisor of the future helps not just with the kids' or grandkids' financial educations or college educations but goes on to help with employment and career track by using his or her contacts to help set up internships or job interviews. He or she works with the family on when and how to pass assets to the next generation—not just by doing estate planning but by becoming the intermediary between generations when it comes to finances and mortality, thereby becoming indispensable to the family. Many advisors list "estate planning" as an additional service, but only advisors of the future have it near the top of the list of services they provide for the same fee.

Another example is bill pay services. The older client finds this tedious and confusing. The advisor of the future will remove that burden and provide that service for the same fee. Some will do it in-house, some will outsource, but they will manage the process and report to the client in a one page monthly report showing what their cash was at the start, what bills were paid, what income came in, what they have at month's end, and how that relates to the plan they agreed to. The advisor of the future is at the center of the client's life.

Investment Alpha Focus on Income Production

Investment management is going to change to accommodate the demographic trends of an aging client base. The shift will be toward strategies that are income-oriented. The advisor of the future will move away from solutions that balance equity and fixed income toward a hypothetical return that meets their financial plan. He or she will talk about how the investments a client is using will produce the income they need to support their lifestyle without running out of resources in their lifetime. The advisor will talk about using strategies that control risk, something older clients can't afford to take at this point in their lives. That advisor controls risk not through a hypothetical lack of correlation that seems to go away in times of crisis but through real strategies to protect/hedge the portfolio's downside.

Investment management is going to change to accommodate the demographic trends of an aging client base.

The advisor of the future won't find these solutions in mainstream offerings. That advisor will need to do the research and understand where the puck is moving.

Team Centered Around Relationship Managers

The advisor of the future will build a team around him or her with RMs that quarterback clients' financial lives so the senior advisor has the time to grow the firm and be a subject matter expert.

RIAs Become Subject Matter Experts and Build Brand

We keep talking about carving out your niche because the successful RIAs of the future will all be subject matter experts. They won't just be generalists in investments; they won't just be financial planners. All will be known for something. They will build a brand—Fisher Investments is a good example—by establishing presence, expertise, and recognition in their niche by using social media, radio, and television.

Industry Moves Toward Hard-Dollar Billing

According to a Wealth X study, "$8.8 trillion [of wealth transfer] … of $15.4 trillion will take place in North America across 360,000 individuals."[43] The advisor of the future that builds the billion-dollar business will focus on these ultrahigh net worth individuals because they have a need you can be a recognized expert in. It's a once-in-a-lifetime niche marketing opportunity that the best advisors will be out ahead. They will be publishing books and articles and then positioning themselves online through SEO to make sure that when these 360,000 of newly minted ultrahigh net worth investors are reaching out and asking questions that their name pops up as a "subject matter expert."[44]

The advisor of the future that builds the billion-dollar business will focus on these ultrahigh net worth individuals because they have a need you can be a recognized expert in.

43 Abby Schultz, "The Wealthy Will Transfer $15.4 Trillion by 2030," *Barron's*, June 26, 2019, https://www.barrons.com/articles/the-wealthy-will-transfer-15-4-trillion-by-2030-01561574217.

44 Samuel Steinberger, "Nearly $9 Trillion Will Change Hands by 2030 in North America," *Wealth Management*, June 28, 2019, https://www.wealthmanagement.com/industry/nearly-9-trillion-will-change-hands-2030-north-america.

Instead of charging a fee on assets under management, the industry is going to move toward hard-dollar billing. An advisor might charge a top client $40K to do asset management and provide a full list of relationship alphas services.

There is far less conflict of interest with this billing structure, and the client wants a crystal-clear view of what they are paying. If an advisor is charging a 1 percent fee on your assets, why would he or she ever suggest the client pay down debt? Although it might be a prudent move, it would lower the advisor's income. Yet we can all agree that paying down debt is something that any financial advisor should be thinking about.

The industry will wake up, realize it's a conflict of interest, and switch to hard-dollar billing. Advisors are going to realize it's better for them too. In 2008, when the market dropped 40 percent, advisors made a lot less while still doing the same job for clients. Hard-dollar billing eliminates that risk for advisors.

Firms Devote Significant Resources to Cyber Security

We believe the advisor of the future is going to devote as much as 5 percent of resources to cyber security, as cyberattacks on businesses with financial data become more commonplace and harder to defend against. Schwab's RIA study reveals that firms are already employing a variety of tactics to protect themselves and their clients from cyber security threats. For example, 90 percent offer employee training, 58 percent have cybersecurity insurance, and 52 percent offer client education to mitigate cyber threats. But the cost as a percentage of revenue is going to increase.

***

We all tend to get in a place where we think we've been through an evolution and know the business. Reality, however, points to drastic demographic and technological changes over the next few decades. Our industry will be very different in ten years. If you follow it, this book is teaching you how to be that advisor of the future. The advisor of the future builds a team with relationship managers delivering relationship alpha. For some advisors out there today, it's going to take a significant strategic shift, but if you want to build a business you can sell half of for $20 million, you will need to do this.

CHAPTER 13

WINNERS MAKE THE MOST MISTAKES

If you've struggled and made mistakes, that means you're trying—not failing. When the legendary college basketball coach John Wooden (who won a record ten NCAA National Championships while coaching UCLA) was a player at Purdue, his coach reinforced the idea that mistakes were the mark of a winner: "The team that makes the most mistakes will probably win." Wooden internalized the message and added his own spin: "The doer makes mistakes," he wrote. "The individual who is mistake-free is also probably sitting around doing nothing."[45]

It was through these mistakes that we learned the right way to grow and be successful in this industry. We made all the mistakes we're warning against in this book, and we still reached $10 million in revenue. If you're stuck at $1–2 million, feel like you're out of time, can't grow, are concerned about quality of life, and want to win, this chapter reviews the steps to break through that wall.

From the outset, you must avoid the tendency that most advisors have to look for shortcuts. We've said this many times throughout the book because it's so important: the grass is simply not greener on

---

45 Stephen Boswell and Kevin Nichols, "Winners Make the Most Mistakes," *Wealth Management*, March 10, 2016, https://www.wealthmanagement.com/business-planning/winners-make-most-mistakes.

the other side. Every ounce of our being wants to achieve success in the quickest way possible. As a result, every advisor will be tempted to take shortcuts—like forming a partnership without really thinking it through (see Chapter 5, "The Risks of Partnerships") or switching firms for a short-term win. Our message is to be very careful about believing the grass is always greener. Usually, it isn't. In our experience, there are no shortcuts to building $10 million in revenue.

In our experience, there are no shortcuts to building $10 million in revenue.

How You Get There

Below is a chapter-by-chapter review of the book focused on the key questions you must consider in order to grow your practice to $1 billion in assets under management and $10 million in annual revenue. With those numbers and the right structure in place, a senior advisor can sell half of that firm for $20 million or more.

Chapter 1: The Things We Wish We'd Known

So many advisors hit the $1–3 million wall because they're spending their time just keeping the business above water. They spend all their working hours with clients and making sure client tasks are achieved, researching investment ideas, making sure their firm is in compliance, or growing the firm through marketing—all jobs their staff should be doing. They just run out of time. As firm owner and senior advisor, you have to be working on the *structure* of the business and growing it, not the day-to-day tasks where you're managing each person's job. Otherwise, you can't scale. You simply can't get to $1 billion AUM, or $10 million in annual revenue, or to monetizing half your business for $20 million without devoting nearly all your working hours to where the business is going and how you get there.

If you're hitting that wall and want to be entrepreneurial but don't know the steps to take to get there, then consider finding a mentor or a consultant who has been there and done all of this. Use their experience and mistakes to guide your path.

Chapter 2: What You Need to Succeed

Do you understand what high performance looks like? This book is not for financial advisors who want to stay in the $1–3 million pack—exactly where most advisors end up spending their careers. We wrote this book for advisors who want to go big and separate themselves from that pack. High-performing firms grow at four times the rate of other firms. Do you possess the eight necessary attributes to reach the high-performing level?

1. Ability to scale. An advisor rising to the high-performing level understands that he or she cannot do everything themselves. They build a team, employ the RM model, and become a specialist.

2. Establishing a specialty. *All* high-performing advisors have a niche. When we became experts in our niche—monetizing a business and setting up a family office—our firm grew exponentially, our ability to price our services effectively improved, and our average account size jumped significantly.

3. Ability to remove client anxiety over money. *All* high-performing advisors have the unique ability to reassure clients facing financial anxiety. They say, "I've been here before, I've seen this before, and here's what you need to do."

4. Connections to new business or outworking the competition. Either you are connected to streams of new business or you

work harder than everyone else. This has been true our entire career. If the average advisor makes *x* efforts to bring in new clients, the high-performing advisor makes 3*x* efforts.

5. Self-confidence. The best advisors have a deep-seated belief in how they invest money. Belief is critical for another reason, too. We're in the business of getting turned down. You've got to have a resilient ego, or it quickly gets old.
6. Integrity. The media loves to throw financial advisors under the bus, but we rarely see a high-performing advisor who didn't have deep integrity. The best advisors *always* put clients first.
7. Conviction. High-performing advisors believe in their experience and their investment philosophy. Conviction comes from having been there and done that at the highest level.
8. Knowing yourself. High-performing advisors meet with clients when they are at their peak. For some advisors, that's morning; for others, it's later in the day. You must know yourself and when you work best because turning prospects into clients requires you to be at peak performance. These advisors work at staying in great physical and mental shape. They work out persistently to deal with the constant stress of our industry.

What if you don't have all these? Find a consultant to help you develop them, or use your peer group where there are advisors who have all these. Watch and emulate them.

Chapter 3: The Best of the Best

Do you understand the difference between lifestyle advisors and enterprise advisors? Have you decided what kind of firm you want?

In an SEI Investments white paper, the authors write that if you don't deliberately decide what kind of firm you want to have, yours will become a lifestyle firm by default. Becoming an enterprise firm requires establishing a "serious and deliberate vision of the kind of firm you are and want to be."[46]

In this chapter, we profile some of the best advisors who helped us learn our way. These advisors all lead enterprise firms, which they've built through scaling, niche marketing, and thinking outside the box. Have you zeroed in on a niche? Do you have deep empathy for your clients and a commitment to lifelong learning? Have you surrounded yourself with a peer group and made the decision to learn from those advisors who are bigger than you? If you surround yourself with the right peer group, learn from people who have been there before you, and use that knowledge to create a story that's unique to you, you can be successful.

Chapter 4: Building the Right Team

Do you understand relationship alpha and value its importance? Today's clients are looking for more than just investment advice. They are looking for holistic services—i.e., advisors who handle their entire financial lives. We know that clients tend to replace their advisors when their financial situation becomes more complex. Matt Oechsli writes, "Possessing the knowledge and

Today's clients are looking for more than just investment advice. They are looking for holistic services—i.e., advisors who handle their entire financial lives.

46 John Anderson, Raef Lee, and Bob Veres, "The Purposeful Advisory Firm," *SEI*, 2017, https://seic.com/sites/default/files/SEI-Purposeful-Advisory-Firm-White-Paper.pdf?cmpid=ADV-FPA-PURPOSE.

professionalism to oversee the complexity of the multidimensional aspects of an affluent client's financial affairs is a basic requirement for working with today's wealth investors. The days of one-dimensional investment advice are over."[47]

To provide relationship alpha, you must have a team around you. There is no possible way to build a firm with $1 billion AUM if you, the owner and senior advisor, are working *in* the business instead of *on* the business. You cannot be CEO, COO, and CIO *and* deliver relationship alpha. It's just not possible. Your relationship managers—the most critical role on your team—handle client relationships. Are your RMs quarterbacking client relationships? Are relationship alpha services part of their job description? Are you paying your team with fixed salaries instead of variable? Do you, the owner and senior advisor, have the role of thought leader?

The sooner advisors start positioning themselves as the quarterback at the center of their clients' lives, the more success they will have in the future. We wish we had recognized much earlier in our career that the most important kind of alpha we provided clients was relationship alpha, not investment alpha. When you start doing everything for clients, the chances of them changing advisors goes down greatly. Relationship alpha has staying power for the future. Equally important, it has pricing power.

What if you don't have a team like this and aren't sure how to get started? Get with someone who does! A consultant or peer who has recognized this and can shepherd the process for you.

---

47 Matt Oechsli, "What Triggers the Affluent to Replace Their Advisor," *Wealth Management*, May 3, 2018, https://www.wealthmanagement.com/prospecting/what-triggers-affluent-replace-their-advisor.

Chapter 5: The Risks of Partnerships

There are many hurdles advisors must clear to get big in this industry. A major hurdle many face is hastily partnering without thinking it through. For the many advisors out there who are hitting the $1–2 million wall, our industry has held up partnerships as the solution. If you're running out of time, standard wisdom tells us to partner with another advisor. Our experience has been different. Forming a partnership creates significant risk for any advisor. In fact, a high percentage of partnerships fail. Do you know the risks? If you do decide to partner, is your partnership structured vertically rather than horizontally? Do you have a written exit strategy agreed upon up front?

If you are in a partnership and see the issue described, how do you get out? Don't try and fail as we did. Use someone with experience to help you find the right solutions because dealing with failed partnerships can kill your productivity for a year or more.

Chapter 6: Clearing the Hurdles

In addition to the lure of partnerships, there are many other hurdles advisors need to overcome in order to get big in this business. Do you have an asset management system that is defensible? Eventually, every advisor out there gets judged on the performance of his or her investments. You simply must be able to defend your strategy to clients and remove the anxiety they are facing over investment performance. Do you have an investment strategy that you believe in and can defend? Do you manage money *only* in that easily defensible way? Do you invest your own money where you invest your clients'?

There are other hurdles as well. You are no longer a financial advisor; you are now a business owner. Have you embraced that role and everything that comes with it? In addition to being the subject matter expert with clients, you now manage people, a P/L, vendors, legal and compliance matters, marketing, branding, and technology. Do you understand the importance of outsourcing these functions until your revenue is high enough to hire people to handle them? Do you cross-check important decisions with your peer group? Do you maintain price integrity? Do you understand how common burnout is in our industry and take time away to recharge? Do you follow a process instead of falling in love with a particular asset manager or financial product? Do you always do what's right for the client, trusting that the rest will work out?

If these questions have mixed answers, hopefully this book has provided usable solutions. However, if you need more support, consultants and peer groups are where you can turn.

Chapter 7: Running Your Practice Like a Business

Have you gone away for a long weekend, turned off your phone, sat down with a pen and paper, and written and rewritten precisely what value you offer clients? Do you have a strategic plan that lays out where you'll be in one year, three years, ten years, and twenty years? Do you track your business monthly and compare it to peer groups? Have you planned for capital expenditures to keep growing? Do you have a dedicated philosophy around paying your team?

Running your practice like business also means planning for a black swan event. "Black swan" is an industry term for a once-in-a-generation event—like 1929, 1987, and 2008. Nine out of ten advisors we meet don't have a plan for a black swan event. Instead, they talk about their investment plan—i.e., how their investments will do during a downturn. But they have no business plan. This is very shocking, considering the quality of the advisors we consult with. Unfortunately, it's extremely common to have no plan at all for a black swan, yet every business should have a plan. Write a plan and be cognizant of it. That way, when the market has a black swan, you won't have to tear apart your business for the two or three-year period, put your own family in financial peril, or lose critically important staff before it comes back.

Finally, do you respect how much strain this business can put on your marriage and family? Sadly, the divorce rate in our industry is well above the national average. We can't even count the number of friends we've had in the industry who worked so hard to build great businesses but, in the process, ruined relationships with their family members. Please make sure to take these words to heart: work as hard on your family as you do on your business. We thank Meg Hirshberg, author of *For Better or For Work: A Survival Guide for Entrepreneurs and Their Families*, for this advice. Don't just pay it lip service. Our friends who got divorced weren't horrible people—they talked about their spouses and kids regularly and had family photos all over their offices—but they didn't take the time to work on their families. They didn't do the kind of planning and goal setting for their families that we do every day in our business. This causes neglect, and, eventually, things fall apart.

Please make sure to take these words to heart: work as hard on your family as you do on your business.

Ask yourself these questions: Have I done the same type of work for my family as I've done for my business? Have we set goals together? Do we meet regularly to measure how we are progressing with those goals? If you feel overwhelmed and need help getting started or writing these plans for your business and family, consultants and peer groups are a great place to turn to.

Chapter 8: How to Grow Your Practice

Have you defined your niche? Growing your practice depends on having a specialty. In order to have a marketing plan that will work, you must know the exact type of client you are going after, and you must be recognized in your niche. Do you know how to get presence? Have you established your reputation in your niche? Do you have a written marketing plan to capitalize on that reputation? It's shocking to see how many advisors do not have a written plan. They know what kind of clients they want, but they haven't dedicated the time to write a detailed marketing plan in which they define the value they provide to that niche, how the message will be delivered, and how it will result in adding more clients. Once you have a plan, do you follow it, measure it, and comp it? At our firm, we had weekly meetings to measure our plan, and we aligned our bonus structure to marketing. The reality is that marketing doesn't just happen; it is a culture that must be developed. Have you taken steps to understand SEO and social media marketing? Do you pay marketing people with fixed salaries, like your team, rather than variable pay? Do you avoid making low pricing a marketing strategy?

The reality is that marketing doesn't just happen; it is a culture that must be developed.

If this sounds like a full-time job and you are thinking you already have one, use a consultant to help you develop the plan and get you started down the path.

Chapter 9: How to Grow Your Practice Through M&A

The last chapter covered organic marketing. While organic growth is important for every advisor out there, do you also understand the power of inorganic growth? Inorganic growth through mergers and acquisitions is such a powerful tool in our business. If we had started pursuing it earlier and not waited until later in our career, it would have cut five or ten years off our timeframe. Had we understood the power of M&A—how, with one purchase, you can make up for five or ten years of prospecting—we would have jumped on it a lot sooner. We would have built our firm differently than we did. We would have built up our resources and RMs (the key to inorganic marketing = capacity) so we could have started acquiring other firms earlier.

Do you understand the keys to M&A success—having the right resources, the right team structure, the right operations system, and the right investment team? Do you have the technology necessary for bulk onboarding of new clients? Do you understand your options for getting the money required to complete a M&A transaction? Are you pursuing firms in your niche with similar beliefs? While most of the industry focuses on the bigger deals, are you aware that smaller M&A transactions can be extremely beneficial? Do you know how to find sellers? In addition to acquisitions, are you aware of the benefits and challenges of mergers? Are you mindful of never taking too much risk with any M&A transaction?

If not, there are people who can help who have been there and built inorganic marketing for firms like yours. Outsource!

Chapter 10: The Choices You Make

Just like in professional sports, advisors are called talent. They can be traded; they can be bought and sold. Are you aware of all your employment options (wire houses, independents, semi-independents, and partnered independents)? Do you understand the benefits and disadvantages of each? Are you aware of current trends in the wire house world—in particular the dismantling of protocol and the increase in advisors leaving wire houses to set up independent shops? Do you understand the economics of monetizing half your book of business for $20 million? Ultimately, the most important question guiding the choices you make is whether you want to be an employee or an entrepreneur. If the latter is correct, then independence might be right for you. If you are going to start your own firm, adhere to the advice in this book about not believing the grass is greener at any other firm.

Either way, using a consultant to evaluate options is critical as exploring these areas is complex and time-consuming.

Chapter 11: How to Make a Graceful Exit

How do you exit your life's work in a graceful way, one that honors your clients and employees? Do you know where to focus to get your ducks in a row to create this kind of exit? One that maximizes your firm's valuation *and* honors the people you've worked with for so many years? Are you both financially and emotionally ready? Have you identified your firm's weaknesses, particularly any holes in infrastructure, and corrected them in order to maximize your valuation? Do you have a story around why you're selling the firm? Have you answered key questions—why won't clients leave, why won't key personnel leave, what are the buyer's risks—before ever meeting with a prospective buyer? Besides selling, what other options do you have for making a graceful exit? Are you aware of economic cycles and mindful of when the timing is right to exit? Are you making sure to leave your staff and clients in good hands?

Chapter 12: What is the Future?

We wrote this book to teach you how to be the advisor of the future. Our industry will be drastically different ten years from now. The average life span is increasing; America's population is aging, retiring, and looking for investments that support their lifestyle rather than grow capital. Are you looking toward where the puck is going, not where it is now? The puck is moving toward advisors being at the center of clients' financial lives. Are you becoming the solution to what clients are worried about?

Other changes are coming too. Can you see how the wire houses are changing as well, offering clients a one-stop shop for asset management, accounting, and lending? Are you positioning your firm to compete in this environment, avoid fee compression, and be able to offer more services under one fee? Are you ready to embrace relationship alpha and be a life coach and financial consultant rolled into one?

In Closing: We Wouldn't Have Changed the Relationships

In order to get to the place of selling half our firm for $20 million, we had to learn from many mistakes. Now, we're teaching from the things we did wrong. Obviously, we would have changed a lot about how we built our business. But there are also things we wouldn't have changed—and they all involve relationships.

Our team. We are extremely proud of the team we built around us. We could not have done it without them. They did a phenomenal job and made incredible contributions to our success and, more importantly, the clients we served. As evidence of the type of people they are, our relationship managers and senior operations staff spent most of their entire careers with us. It's very unusual in our industry for RMs to have that kind of tenure with one firm.

Our clients. It was such an honor to work alongside our clients, realizing their dreams of selling a lifetime's worth of work, cashing in, and checking that financial box that says, "I'm done." It was deeply rewarding to help clients build family offices, put in place succession planning, and work with the kids as they became successful—due to the groundwork that was laid by the family office. We would not have changed any of that. We loved every second of it.

We would not have served a different set of clients. A lot of advisors look back and say, "I wish we would have handled bigger clients" or "I wish we would have done foundations and endowments." In contrast, we've truly loved being a part of our clients' lives. It has impacted us deeply to be a part of their lives. The feeling of a client suddenly seeing the light or the solution to a problem—not because we were smarter but because they were too close to the situation—has been incredibly rewarding. When a client understood that there was an achievable, executable path to solving their problem(s), it proved to be a gratifying experience for everyone involved and not just a job.

There's one other thing about working with clients we would not have changed: relentlessly putting the client first. We're very proud that clients' interests *always* came first in our practice—not 99 percent of the time but 100 percent. Although it's clearly the right thing to do, it's hard to adhere to in day-to-day practice. But we did so consistently. It may have cost us money multiple times, but as we look back, we would not have changed that in the slightest.

Our peer group. We would not have chosen to be involved with a different peer group. When we were at "the wall," there were few consultants who had actually gone to that $10 million mark in billables we sought. There is simply no way we would have gotten where we did without the relationships we built at the Association of Professional Investment Consultants. Find a peer group that works for you and build those relationships. We followed advisors who were bigger than us—we had people to emulate, a "been there, done that" model. Then we could put our own twist on it.

***

John Wooden's wisdom has guided us for many years: "Winners make the most mistakes." You can't be afraid to fail in this business. You're going to do some things that won't succeed. You're going to hire some people who don't work out. You're going to reach a point where you're spending your last dollar and hoping it works. We were right there with you at all those stages. The real winners keep coming back. If you need help to put all this in place, seek out peers or consultants who have been there and done that to show you the way because it is achievable!

CPSIA information can be obtained
at www.ICGtesting.com
Printed in the USA
BVHW090035171221
624207BV00016B/871

9 781949 639513